Potbellied Pigs
In Your Home

TS-208

Distributed in the UNITED STATES to the Pet Trade by T.F.H. Publications, Inc., One T.F.H. Plaza, Neptune City, NJ 07753; distributed in the UNITED STATES to the Bookstore and Library Trade by National Book Network, Inc. 4720 Boston Way, Lanham MD 20706; in CANADA to the Pet Trade by H & L Pet Supplies Inc., 27 Kingston Crescent, Kitchener, Ontario N2B 2T6; Rolf C. Hagen Ltd., 3225 Sartelon Street, Montreal 382 Quebec; in CANADA to the Book Trade by Macmillan of Canada (A Division of Canada Publishing Corporation), 164 Commander Boulevard, Agincourt, Ontario M1S 3C7; in ENGLAND by T.F.H. Publications, PO Box 15, Waterlooville PO7 6BQ; in AUSTRALIA AND THE SOUTH PACIFIC by T.F.H. (Australia), Pty. Ltd., Box 149, Brookvale 2100 N.S.W., Australia; in NEW ZEALAND by Brooklands Aquarium Ltd. 5 McGiven Drive, New Plymouth, RD1 New Zealand; in Japan by T.F.H. Publications, Japan—Jiro Tsuda, 10-12-3 Ohjidai, Sakura, Chiba 285, Japan; in SOUTH AFRICA by Multipet Pty. Ltd., P.O. Box 35347, Northway, 4065, South Africa. Published by T.F.H. Publications, Inc.

MANUFACTURED IN THE UNITED STATES OF AMERICA
BY T.F.H. PUBLICATIONS, INC.

POTBELLIED PIGS IN YOUR HOME

DENNIS KELSEY-WOOD

Photo Credits

A very special thanks to the following contributors whose photographs appear on the pages indicated.

Anita Beeman, 32; Betty Beeman, 43, 70 150; Jenny Blaney, 28, 39, 85, 93, 106, 108, 110 115, 121, 124, 130, 145, 157, 153, 155; Jim Carroccio, 13, 75, 79, 80, 135, 151; Gail DeJongh, 11, 19, 45, 48, 91, 127; Shalisa Faulk, 31; Nancy Goshorn 20, 21, 25, 53, 69, 79, 89; Jane Hall, 30, 100, 114; Heather Kingdon, 48, 51, 59, 83, 95, 143; Lyons Family, 50, 103; Gary Moore, 29, 33, 40, 42, 47, 54; Sarnan Publishing, 1, 3, 7, 8, 9, 12, 14, 15, 18, 24, 26, 27, 35, 41, 46, 52, 56, 58, 62, 63, 64, 68, 71, 72, 77, 78, 82, 84, 90, 92, 94, 96, 97, 98, 99, 102, 107, 111, 116, 117, 119, 122, 125, 126, 126, 128, 129, 133, 134, 137, 138, 141, 142, 144, 146, 149, 152, 157; Karen Taylor, 17, 23, 36, 38, 55, 57, 61, 65, 72, 73, 86, 86, 87, 105, 109, 112, 120, 123, 123, 131, 139, 148; Jane Treser, 37, 136.

The following piggeries are acknowledged for providing some of the photographs used in this book:

Beeman Farms, Garlyn Farm, Good Day Ranch, Ham-A-Lot-Village, Lil' Lightnin' Ranch, Lil' Pigs' Top Brass, Petite Pigs For Pets, Precious Porkers Oink., The Lyons Den, The Source, Tuffenuf Acres.

Contents

Introduction

When Keith Connell, a Canadian zoo director, decided to import a number of Vietnamese potbellied pigs into his country, little did he realize that within just a few years these pigs would be the new smash-hit pet of the 1990s. There is, of course, nothing new about pigs being kept as pets because their appeal has spanned centuries in just about every country in the world. However, most porcine pals have lived on farms in western countries, or in the villages and shanty towns of Third World countries.

Those who have kept pigs purely as pets, and not for their bacon or pork chops, have always been regarded as being a rather bizarre group of people. After all, how could anyone love a large, ungainly 1,000-lb. creature that grunts continually, churns everything into a mudhole, is blessed with a decidedly dubious nature, and revels in making its home a real pigsty—smell and all.

We all know that porkies are reputedly very intelligent animals and play an important role in the farming policies of most national economies. But the pig's ever becoming a big-time pet, that's another matter. Sure, if pigs could fly, it might happen.

Well, you had better keep your eyes on the skies because the Vietnamese potbellied pig must have sprouted wings—it really has established itself as the pet of thousands of people living in both rural and urban areas. More than that, it resides in the home of its owner, not in a barnyard or pigsty.

The new "in" pet has been raised to a level never before dreamed of. Many sleep on a king- or queen-size bed alongside their owners at night. If they do not, there is a good chance they have their own large beanbag or other luxury bed in the living room. They are coddled, groomed, and pampered just like the best of dogs, cats, or children. A whole commercial industry is frantically being developed to try and cash in on these boom pets. Whether it be making harnesses, jackets, fancy clothes, sweatshirts for the owners, piggy mugs, or piggy greeting cards, it seems that if it features porky, it's a winner. There are special foods for potbellies, and these princely porkers even have their own glossy magazine to enthrall their owners with what is happening in the high-speed world of this new star.

The potbelly has its own registration associations and can be exhibited at its own special shows. There are even graduation classes being organized so that porky will be educated in the more gentile ways of living among humans. It's enough to make any self-respecting dog or cat wonder what is happening in the world today! So what is this high-priced bacon all about, and what special charms does it have that have enabled it to take the pet world by storm in such a short period of time?

The fact that you are reading this text suggests that you are one of the thousands of people that have heard about this new pet, or maybe you have already been captivated having seen one or more of them and now want to find out if you too could become an owner. If you have not already obtained a potbellied pig, then you have made the right decision to look into matters first.

Pet potbellied pigs enjoy being spoiled and fussed over, as do many pet dogs and cats.

The Vietnamese potbelly is a miniature as porkies go. This is the basic reason why it has been such a whirlwind success. Its other virtues are exactly the same as those of its larger cousins that have enthralled those who have been hog-tied to them over the centuries.

In this book, the object is not simply to sell you on the idea of owning a potbelly but to give you solid practical advice on what is entailed in caring for these delightful pets. As with any other animal that suddenly finds itself in the limelight, there is always a great deal of misinformation bandied about it. There are those who climb on the bandwagon for no other reason than to make money off of the pet. They extol its virtues while practicing any means that they can to part you from the largest amount of cash.

Sadly, there are always many people who will hand over their hard-earned money without having the slightest inclination of what problems they may come up against. It may seem amazing that a person would hand over a few hundred dollars and take possession of a pig without even knowing how to feed it! But this really does happen. So much heartache and misery could be avoided if potential owners would take at least a little time to ask basic questions about a pet that must still be regarded as being an exotic, even if it is so well-known an animal.

It could be said that those who

become disenchanted owners have only themselves to blame for rushing in without seeking proper advice. This is so for a number of people who obtain pets simply as status symbols, or because it seems a good way to draw attention to themselves, or to make some quick cash. But that still leaves a lot of well-intentioned people who are told only the positive side about potbellies and not what sort of problems they might encounter and how they can be resolved. Not every person is suited to owning these porky pets, no more than every person is suited to owning a dog, a cat, or a parrot.

Any pet carries with it a need for the owner to take a responsible stance on its care. The need for responsibility is at its peak when deciding if it is fair to take the animal into the household in the first place. It is not simply a case of whether you have the cash or the space to accommodate a potbelly but whether you have the willingness to devote to it the special attention that it needs in certain aspects of its care. Obviously, it cannot be compared to a dog, a cat, a horse, or a rabbit.

For many thousands of people, the potbellied pig has proved to be the ultimate pet. But for a number of others, it has proved a disaster that could so easily have been avoided by simply holding back and checking out the problems as well as the benefits of actual ownership. Once you have determined that the potbelly is for you and your family, then you will find within these chapters all the basic information that is available at this time on how to ensure that you are truly delighted with your pet.

Being such a new pet, there is still much to be learned about these delightful little porkers. So even as a newcomer to pigs, it is quite possible that you may be able to contribute to the advancement of information on them. Thus, they are exciting pets to own not simply because of their own fascination but because each new

These miniature cousins of the well known barnyard pigs are steadily becoming established as household pets.

These pets enjoy living at a leisurely pace. A comfortable place to rest will be much appreciated and enjoyed.

owner can contribute to their future development as an established pet. In a few years, they may be regarded in the same manner as are the other animals that we accept as being suited to living alongside us and sharing our homes.

The way potbellies are perceived by other pet owners and the public at large will be determined by how each owner cares for the piggy that he takes into his home.

Problems and Virtues

For many people, the decision on whether or not to purchase a given pet animal is often made in a manner that does not compare with the way they might normally go about obtaining any other item, be it a home, a car, or even a household article. Where pets are concerned, an element of total mental irrationality may influence decisions. If you are purchasing a new car, you will no doubt consider whether or not a given model is suited to your needs in respect to its size, seating, and initial cost. How much gas will it burn? Does it have a good resale value? Are parts easy to obtain? What will it cost to insure? You will not rush out and purchase the first one of the desired model that you see advertised but will visit showrooms—perhaps even private homes—so that you can compare one vehicle with the next. You will also have pondered whether or not it will fit into your garage or driveway. Thus, in one way or another, you will have given very much thought to many aspects of that vehicle. If you need a pickup truck, it is unlikely you will purchase a sports car. As much as you may like a sporty two-seater, you are wise enough to appreciate that such a vehicle will not meet your needs.

When many owners decide to bring new pets into their homes, they seem to be totally focused on the fact that they want a particular pet—to the degree that all other aspects are overlooked.

It is enough for them that they are fascinated by the pet and are totally captivated by how it looks as a little baby. Their heart overrides their normal common sense approach to ownership.

In the following text I will relate many of the real problems in owning a potbellied pig—as well as its many virtues. You are strongly advised to consider in depth the problems. If you can genuinely accept them as realities (rather than pay lip service to them), then you will clearly have no concerns as to the virtues of these captivating little creatures. If the potential problems cause you not to go ahead with obtaining a potbelly, then the text will have achieved its objective. It will also have saved you a great deal of money, a lot of heartache, and will also have saved a little pig from a lot of distress.

THE LEGAL STATUS OF A POTBELLY

Many pets, such as fish, mice, small birds, and hamsters, have no legal-status problems associated with their ownership. That is to say they are rarely, if ever, the subject of specific ordinances that restrict their being kept within a domestic environment. Dogs, more so than cats, are subject to such restrictions, but in general they are accepted as being household pets. Thus, they may be kept in homes, providing certain local regulations regarding noise, disturbance, and any outdoor housing are complied with.

Potbellied pigs, at this point in time, are invariably outside of the realm of those animals accepted as domestic pets. As cute as they may be, they are regarded as farm livestock by most local authorities. They are swine and thus are subject to regulations applicable to swine. What does this mean?

1. Swine are subject to local farm

Before purchasing a new pet, whether it be a potbellied pig, dog or bird, do some research to find out what is entailed in keeping and caring for your new companion.

livestock health regulations.

This means that they must be vaccinated according to local requirements, which are based on commercial herds—not on the single-pet home situation. The fact that a pet potbelly will not be in an environment where many potential swine diseases could arise is neither here nor there from a legal standpoint. When the regulations were made, they were made from a commercial viewpoint of health safety: pet pigs were not even considered because no one kept a pig in his home.

2. Swine are subject to transportation restrictions, so they cannot be taken from one locality to another with the same ease as is the case with a dog or a cat. In the USA and Australia, you may interpret locality as being from state to state. In the UK, it may be county to county. In any event, if there is an outbreak of a major swine disease, even in a very local area, the movement of swine from one place to

another may be banned or very restricted. In order to transport a potbelly across a state border, it must meet with state vaccination requirements, as well as have a current certificate of health. Not all vets in urban areas are willing to attend to these needs, which means you may need to locate a vet who handles farm livestock.

3. Swine are subject to restrictions of housing. This means that a given local authority may require that the accommodations be constructed of certain materials and meet other requirements as to the disposal of fecal matter and general health standards. Plans and permissions will normally be required.

4. The number of swine kept in a given accommodation is subject to regulations, as are swine kept for breeding purposes.

The regulations to be complied with vary from state to state and country to country, so this text cannot be specific. Some states make no specific reference to the keeping of farm livestock as domestic pets; others forbid it within domestic home situations. It is thus prudent to check what the regulations are in your immediate locality. You should also consider the legal requirements of taking your pet pig across state lines for the purposes of vacations or exhibition—if they are likely to be considerations. If you fail to take account of these facts, you must accept the consequences of your own actions down the line if problems result.

Many potbellies are more than just pets –they're part of the family, partaking in all activities.

PET ORDINANCES

The foregoing regulations were designed for farm livestock kept in numbers with the end view that they would be slaughtered to provide food for human consumption. They protect you and others in your locality from a neighbor acquiring a half-dozen hogs, sheep, or cows and keeping them in his yard with all the attendant noise, smells, and obvious problems that would be entailed. The arrival of the potbellied pig as a pet has clearly created a need for many local authorities to at least review, and maybe even change, pet-keeping ordinances.

Many potbelly owners keep these animals as pets in contradiction to local ordinances. In some instances, local authorities never make an issue about this unless a person, for whatever reason, decides to challenge the fact that someone is keeping a potbelly within a city limit or in contradiction of livestock regulations. Some authorities are not keen to have their ordinances challenged in courts of law; others have no specific references to the keeping of potbellies. All of this means that the potbelly is having to fight for a redefined status as a pet.

In areas where it has been given pet status, the following are a few of the stipulations that may form part of ordinances:

1. There may be an upper-weight limit that determines whether or not a pig is in fact a miniature pig. This will probably be in the area of 100 lbs.

2. Pet pigs may need to be from proven registered stock.

3. There may be regulations stating that pigs may not be bred within urban limits. In the event that this should happen, it is probable that the regulations will state that the sow must be taken outside of the town limits in order to rear the piglets.

4. Pigs kept as pets in homes must be spayed or neutered.

5. Pet pigs must have their tusks surgically removed.

6. Pet pigs must be vaccinated against communicable diseases common within the species.

7. Pet pigs must be licensed with the local authority and a given annual fee paid.

8. There is normally a limit to the number of pigs that may be kept as household pets. This may be as low as a single pig.

9. Pet pigs will be required to be restrained on a leash at all times when outside of their home environment.

There will also probably be references to requirements for outside enclosures, which shall not be allowed to become muddy, messy, or in other ways offensive to others within the neighborhood.

From the foregoing it is obvious that if you wish to have no problems in the keeping of a potbellied pig, it would be prudent to check what the situation is in your area. If the pig

There may be certain regulations in your area that you will need to be aware of when keeping potbellied pigs. This cat is investigating the new kids on the block.

does not have pet status, the next thing to do is to inquire if your local authority has on its schedule any discussions that might involve the review of pet ordinances. If not, maybe there are other owners in the area, and maybe they are planning to bring amendments to the attention of your local governing body.

Help in drafting proposals for amended ordinances can be obtained via numerous sources. They include local or other vets, national associations, and established breeders who have been involved in preparing proposals in their own localities. You may also seek the help of your local officials if they are known to be sympathetic to pet-pig ownership. Be sure that if you purchase a potbellied pig, it complies with the ordinances likely to be applicable to it.

I should add to this question of legality of ownership the following: Some members of the public have purchased pet pigs locally from breeders, dealers, and pet shops on the assumption that if they can be sold, they can therefore be kept as pets. This is not so. Let us consider pet shops. They are licensed to sell animals, be they domestic or exotic, providing they meet whatever regulations are applicable to pet shops in your area. This does not mean that all of the animals sold may legally be kept as pets in that area. An exotic animal dealer in your area may include elephants in the inventory, but you would hardly expect to be able to take one home as a pet! The laws in respect to selling, breeding, and the keeping of animals as pets are unrelated to each other.

Finally, in the event that you should find yourself being served a citation that says you are in violation of an ordinance, you should not give up your pig without a fight. It is possible that local ordinances are not being interpreted correctly by town

Whenever out of the house or yard, pigs should be harnessed and leashed.

Although your piglet is cute and innocent, without proper early training it can grow to be an unmanageable adult.

hall. You may be able to challenge the citation and may interest your local newspapers in your case. Such press support will bring focus on the situation and may result in the whole question being examined and the wording of bylaws changed in favor of pet-pig ownership. It is altogether better to try and challenge town hall before the fact rather than after it.

YOUR TIME FACTOR

A question you must address fairly in respect to keeping any pet, and especially a little piglet, is that regarding the time you will be able to devote to it. If you and other members of your household will be away for most of the day, is it really fair to introduce a very social animal into a situation where it will be left to its own devices most of the time? The answer must be a definite "no." Further, if you like to get away on weekends, will you be able to take porky with you? If not, then all of this means that the all-important close ties with your porcine friend will be missing. This will usually result in a difficult pet to manage and one that will not be a happy little companion.

Ownership of any intelligent creature such as a pig should be a two-way deal in which both gain from the situation. If it is based on the notion that because you want a given pet is justification enough to own one, this is a very one-sided arrangement that suggests an inconsiderate person.

FEEDING POTBELLIED PIGS

It is not satisfactory to feed your porcine pet on standard commercial pig foods. All miniature pigs require specialized diets if they are to be maintained in the best of health. There is no problem obtaining such foods, but you may have to obtain them via mail order or travel a little

A favored treat for all potbellies –GRAPES!

farther than normal in order to locate a seller who stocks them. Clearly, your best approach is to discuss your needs with your local pet shop dealer.

Pet-pig feeds will progressively become more readily available as potbellies and other miniature pigs gain popularity, but at this time you must accept the fact that initially you may have to shop around for a supplier.

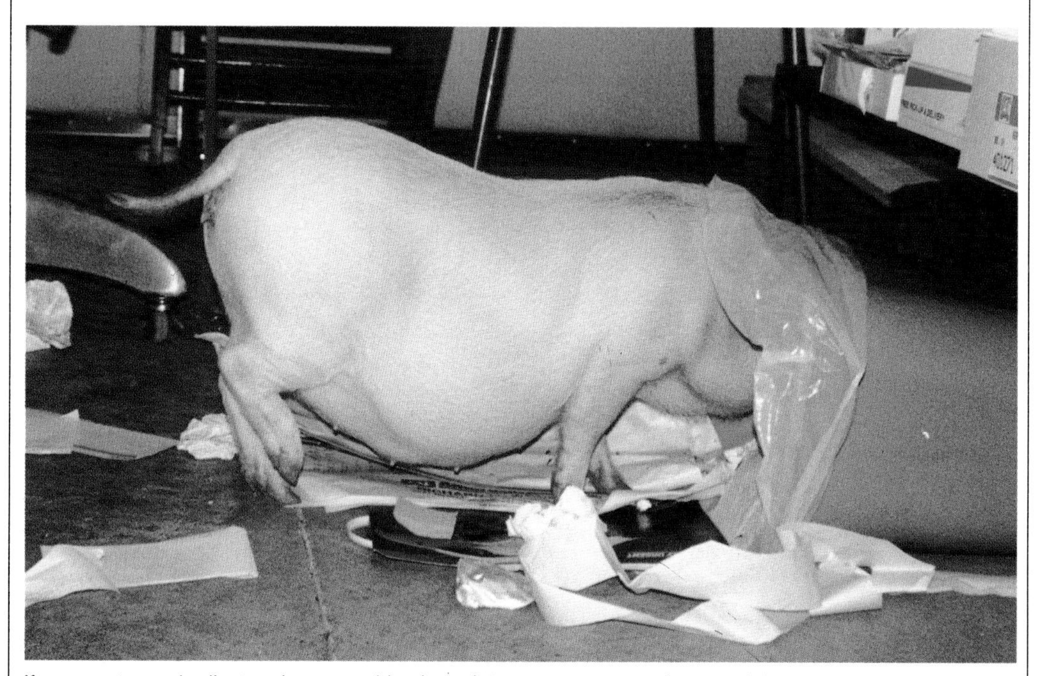

If one wants an obedient and manageable pig, training at an early age is essential.

TRAINING

Pigs are extremely intelligent animals, and this can prove to be a double-edged sword if you do not have the willingness and character to be capable of training them in the basics of living in your home. A delinquent pig can soon become the source of considerable worry to you. Among the problems some owners have experienced are the following: aggressiveness when porky is not getting his own way, biting strangers and family members (including other pets), charging at strangers and other animals, difficulty in housetraining them in their toiletry needs, damaging furniture, and excessive squealing when they do not get their own way. Further, some piglets, due to incorrect early socialization, can be extremely nervous. Unless this matter is overcome by patient handling, the youngster will grow up to be a very difficult pet to manage.

In reality, the potential problems that are inherent with a pig are not so different than those seen in unruly dogs. The difference is that the average person is aware that a large dog can be dangerous, whereas this aspect is not so widely appreciated where a miniature pig is concerned. There is also no denying that litter-box training a pig is not quite as easy as it is with cats.

If you are the kind of person who has a small dog that literally rules your household and would be a real menace were it not for its small size, it is likely you would have major problems with a potbellied pig. You must be very honest with yourself when considering a mini pig because it is, in spite of its small size, a very powerful creature that is clever enough to work out how to get its own way with a person who does not have the strength of character to control it. This does not imply that pigs need hard handling; they need quite the reverse. They react to affection, but they must be given regular training in just the same way as must a Rottweiler, Doberman, or similar powerful canine.

GENERAL HOME LIFE

A potbellied pig is neither a large pet nor is it unduly heavy when compared to many dog breeds. However, it may appear so because its weight is channeled into four small hard hooves.

The result is that an adult pig can easily damage chairs, sofas, or beds by the pressure exerted through the hooves. Nor is a pig the most nimble of creatures when moving from one place to another.

It does not like climbing stairs, and it is not at all sure-footed on any surface that is slippery, such as tiled or polished wood floors.

Pigs have never been blessed with eating etiquette; they often slobber, and they eat their food with very obvious relish. If you prefer the delicate manners of a feline in your pet, then you will be sadly disillusioned with a pig. Finally, whether male or female, I can guarantee dissatisfaction with a potbelly as a house pet if it is not neutered or spayed.

There is no animal that can be said to be the perfect pet because each one has some attendant problems that must be addressed. If the pet is

A potbelly should not be dealt with in a harsh manner. It reacts and learns better when shown lots of attention and affection.

small, such as a mouse, hamster, or rabbit, the problems rarely create any difficulty in being overcome. As the pet gets larger, there is a greater need for the owner to be more involved with it. The millions of dogs and cats, as well as horses, large parrots, and other pets, that are abandoned and placed in animal shelters or passed on to other unsuspecting owners are testimony to the fact that their owners simply did not consider the hard realities of owning them in the first place. Do not be tempted to purchase a potbellied pig just because it looks so cute as a piglet. A potbelly is not a pet that should be acquired without a great deal of realistic thought.

Piglets are curious and gentle creatures. They get along well with most other family pets.

THE VIRTUES OF POTBELLIED PIGS

Probably the singular reason that any person feels a desire to own a given animal species is that he finds it appealing. This, more than other virtues, is the cornerstone of a desire to want to form a relationship with an animal. After all, the fact that another creature may be less costly, more practical in its management, or more cuddly, will not sway you from pig ownership if you have decided you want a potbelly. What you perceive as a virtue may not be regarded as such by another pet owner, or even by a pig owner. This accepted, the following are but a few advantages to owning a porcine pet.

As stated earlier, pigs are highly intelligent creatures, which means that given the correct care and training, they will form extremely strong bonds with you and others in your family. Their natural intelligence enables them to be trained to a very high degree, which is both fun and a challenge to you. They are very amusing creatures and fit amazingly well within a domestic environment. The only reason they may appear out of place is because the majority of people are simply not familiar with them.

As pigs mature, they slow down dramatically; and this can be a decided advantage if you are the type who prefers a more sedate pet. On its daily excursion for exercise, your porcine pal will not drag you at high speed around the block. Indeed, it will move around at the rate of speed that might see you nodding off! Pigs like to go through life at a very leisurely pace.

Unlike dogs and cats, pigs are rarely infested with lice or fleas because they have little hair in which parasites can hide and multiply. Contrary to their popular image, pigs are extremely clean animals that have no undue odor (if they are neutered). The image of smelly, dirty creatures that enjoy wallowing in mud is derived from the fact that under commercial environments they are often forced to live in dirty, inadequate conditions. Further, pigs are rather sensitive to heat, a result of which is that if such a situation is not overcome, they will wallow in any kind of water (thus create mud) in order to cool their bodies. The fecal matter of pigs is, in fact, less offensive to your nostrils than that of dogs, cats—or humans! This is because it contains less ammonium compounds, which in the species mentioned are a result of the higher protein content of their diets.

Pigs will make friends with any other pets that you may own because they are essentially very gregarious by nature. They live in herds in the wild so they have a need to form social bonds. If these bonds are not with their own species, pigs simply adopt whatever other animals are living with them; and these other animals are treated as their own kind. This means you, your family, and your other pets.

No animal should ever be purchased in order to be projected as a status symbol. Having said this, the fact is that if you love pigs, you will find that as a side benefit lots of people will want to talk to you when you are out walking with porky. If you are one of those people who are rather shy at meeting other people, you will find that your pet will help to "break the ice". Everyone is fascinated by a piggy on a leash and will want to ask you questions about it.

While dogs and cats may become very finicky eaters that cause you to worry over them, this is not likely to be a problem with a potbelly. Potbellies' legendary love of all foods is well deserved, and this means that if you run out of their special diet you will never be at a loss over what to give them. Indeed, so voracious is their appetite that one of the major problems with these pets is that unless you carefully regulate their eating habits, they can quickly become obese, which is bad for their health.

Most of all, potbellied pigs are simply very, very lovable pets that just want to be with you. This, after all, is what a perfect pet is all about and the reason why so many thousands of people have found the potbelly to be the answer to their pet needs.

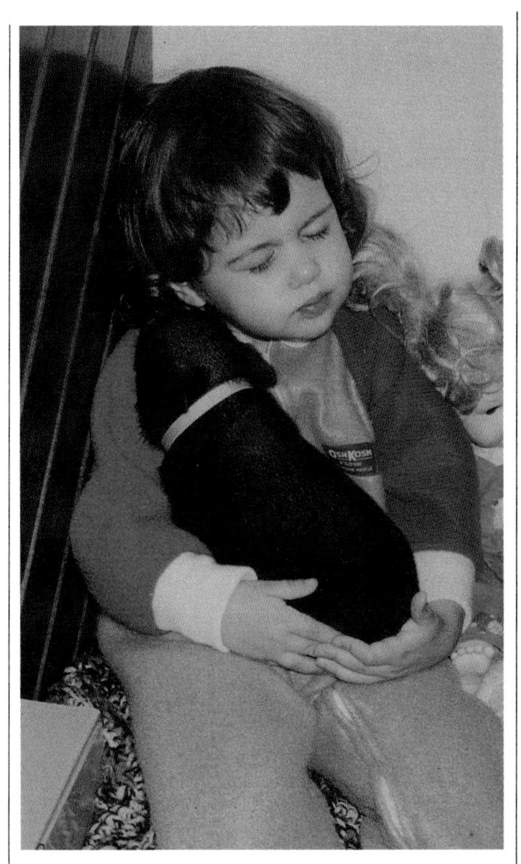

Pigs love to cuddle. These two pals decided to snuggle up and take a nap together.

Finally, they are reasonably long lived. At present, no one is exactly sure what their upper-age potential is because up until this time no one has kept them as pets for more than a few years. They have lived for fifteen years in zoos, so it can be assumed that an average lifespan will be on the order of ten to fifteen years, with a potential to reach a few more years under ideal conditions.

Purchasing a Potbelly

Having carefully considered all of the points discussed in the previous chapter, and having satisfied yourself and your family that you will provide a really loving home for little porky, there will no doubt be many questions for which you will be wanting answers. For example, which sex should you have, which color, what age is best, what price should you pay? Because there are so many things for you to think about, the first golden rule when purchasing any pet is never to rush into it. This really is very sound advice when related to a potbellied pig at this stage in the development of the pet pig market.

POT-BELLIED PIGS MAGAZINE AND ASSOCIATIONS

Those involved with the potbellied pig are very fortunate that so early on in the development of this pet there is a glossy magazine devoted to it, as well as national associations. It would, therefore, make a great deal of sense to subscribe to the magazine and join an association as part of your information-gathering process. Apart from all of its excellent articles, the publication also carries many breeder and useful-item advertisements. It is an invaluable tool in gaining much background information about the whole potbellied scene. The same is equally true of the associations, which provide a number of services. Take a month or more over your selection process, and during this time the articles that you read will give you a "feel" for the whole scene.

SIZE AND WEIGHT

The maximum shoulder height of a Vietnamese potbellied pig is 46cm (18 in.) at the age of 52 weeks, but the desired target height for the future is 36cm (14 in.) or under. The weight range is 40 to 70 lbs. at one year of age, and it may remain at this amount in an adult. But it can climb as high as 150 lbs. in a fully mature specimen. Much attention is being given to breeding smaller and lighter pigs, but you are advised not to place too much importance on these parameters in your pet—always assuming it has been bred from genuine potbellied stock.

There is in all animals a correlation between miniaturization and health and breeding problems. At this time, the data on these aspects is not well documented in potbellies because of the relatively short time that these pigs have been popular pets. Undue efforts to breed for small size without carefully documenting adverse health effects has no merit. The prudent attitude must be that small is best only if there is ample background data to suggest that it is not accompanied by any known defects. Beware of advertisements claiming very small-size breeding stock. Such animals are often immature specimens so they are no guide as to the eventual height of their offspring.

Try to see firsthand the parents of your chosen pet, and, better still, try to contact other pig owners whose pets have the same parents as your pet. In this way, you will get a reasonably good idea of likely ultimate size, weight, and health of the piglet that you choose. There is no benefit in owning a tiny pig if it is

It is important to know the pedigree of a potbelly you wish to purchase to ensure that it is truly a miniature pig and not its farmyard cousin.

chronically ill, so always take a flexible approach to size and weight. Health and disposition are far more important to you. You will not notice if your pet is an inch or two taller than the smallest specimens or if it is a few pounds heavier. But you will be aware if it has a poor nature or is forever suffering from problems that are a direct result of its very small size.

COLOR

The original color of the first potbellied pig imports was black.

Today you can choose from numerous shades ranging from bicolors to whites to silvers. In theory, there is no relationship between color and the quality of the pig, so it is a feature that is important only from a subjective viewpoint. Whites and bicolors are very popular at this time, but do not be swayed by trends. Choose your pet on the basis of its health and disposition. The old adage that a good horse can never be a bad color is very sound advice.

If, however, you plan to become a breeder, there might be merit in considering the fact that the black potbelly is losing some ground to other colors. This is to be expected in any pet once it becomes established and develops color varieties. The comment in respect to color and quality being unrelated in theory should be expanded upon. The reality is that because there is no particular gene relationship between color and quality, it follows that a really outstanding color may be seen in what is otherwise a rather mediocre specimen. When this happens, a color breeder has little option but to use the well-colored specimen, then try and improve any defects over a given breeding-program term.

Given this fact, it follows that the standard of excellence in blacks will tend to always be higher than in specimens of other colors simply because a breeder does not have to compromise on quality.

Good black potbellies will therefore always be well sought after.

WHICH SEX?

From a purely practical-pet viewpoint, it matters not which sex you choose: both are delightful. Of course, you will tend to find that some owners and breeders may claim that one sex is superior to the other. A breeder may try to convince you simply because he has males or females to sell at that moment. Once either sex is rendered incapable of breeding, its basic sex drives change. It is the sex drives that obviously create the major differences between the sexes. If they are removed, the differences are minor, at best, and the nature of your pet will be more of a reflection of how you care for it than of its gender.

From purely personal observations across many pet species, if I had to make a choice between the sexes from a pet viewpoint, I would opt for a male. Males tend to be more confident in themselves and the world around them. They are more happy-go-lucky as a result. The fact that a female has to care for her offspring means she is

Whether you choose a male or a female, if not planning to breed, it should be spayed or neutered.

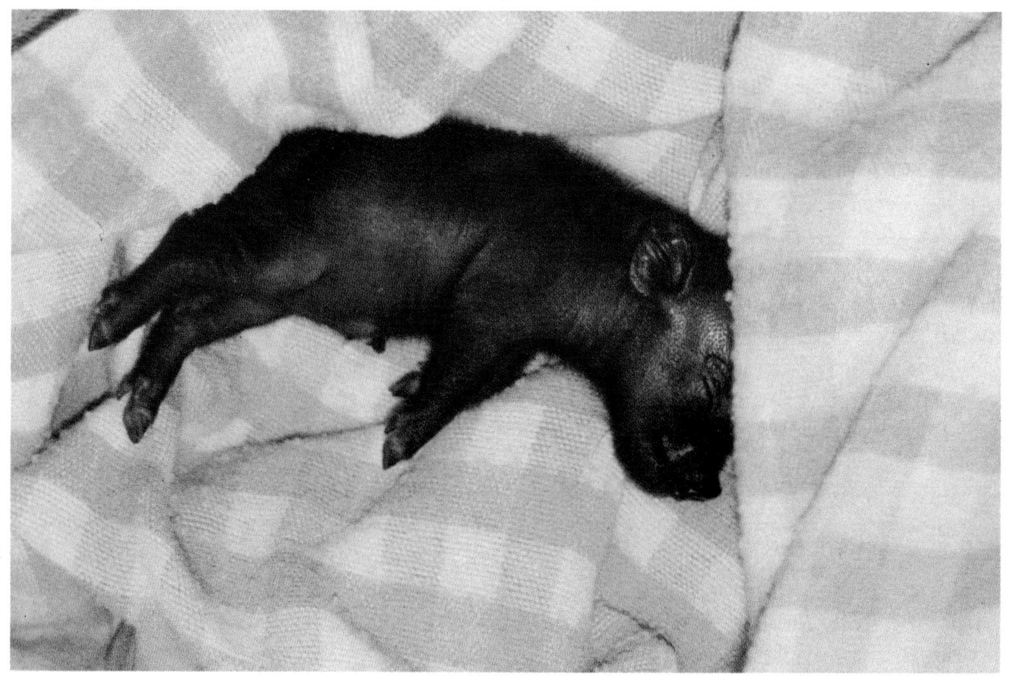

innately more cautious in her relationships. She may be slower in becoming aggressive, but once she has reached that state she tends to be really mean and unforgiving. But if she is cared for with tenderness, she will not display that side of her nature. It could then be said that, unlike the male, she has no desire to take the macho view that "I'm the boss." Thus you are back to the factor of how you care for the potbelly as being the most influential.

It is important that neutering and spaying be effected at an early age. This is true for a number of reasons. First, if either procedure is done at a young age, the cost will be lower. It is more straightforward for a vet to remove the reproductive organs of a female before she has developed extensive layers of fat. The same is true, but to a much lesser degree, with a male.

If the desexing is left until the piglet is older, the pet will be much more difficult to housetrain. Further, the mere surgical act of removing reproductive organs does not mean that the pet will change its nature overnight. Sex drives will, of course, begin diminishing rapidly. However, the habits that were a consequence of sexuality may take weeks or months to change, depending on the age at which the desexing takes place.

Desexing can be done at any age, but pet pigs should be attended to while they are juveniles. The male can be neutered at any age from three weeks and over. The female is best spayed, based on available data, at about six weeks of age, which may also be the ideal time to neuter a male. Any earlier or later than this, the surgery is somewhat more difficult and thus more costly.

Returning to the question of sex, if you have an eye to becoming a breeder, then the female has to be the better choice. Be aware that while she may make a nice yard-pet, she will not be suited to indoor life. The same is equally true of a boar. An unspayed sow will go through her sex cycle every 21 days on average. At such times her disposition will change, and she will be far less predictable. Both sexes will tend to forget all about their toiletry-training habits and eliminate wherever they please. A boar will have a characteristic odor and will be much more aggressive and self-assertive than will the neutered male.

As a breeder, you can select a stud boar from the best in the country and even utilize artificial insemination. It would be a very costly undertaking to obtain a boar that would be suited to your breeding program. The potential breeder thus needs one or more very sound sows on which to base his future program.

The perfect age to acquire a piglet is when it is between 10-12 weeks old, at which time it should already be accustomed to humans.

WHAT AGE?

Never be tempted to purchase a piglet under the age of 8 weeks. Such piglets will barely have been weaned. A good age would be about 10-12 weeks. By this age the youngster will be eating well, will have been neutered or spayed, and will have received all of its vaccinations. It should also have been housetrained and carefully socialized to humans. Each of these factors is a very important consideration with a potential pet that is probably going into a home where the owners have no previous experience with these animals. It is a fact of life that the mortality rate in very young pigs is high, so the more established youngster is the better choice.

Bring a newly purchased pig to a vet to make sure it is healthy. It should be agreed upon before hand with the seller that you may return the pig if this is not the case.

If you plan to be a breeder, the age at which you purchase your sows is more flexible because they will not be living with you in your home. Factors such as quality and price will be important considerations, and they will be influenced by age. For example, the cheapest breeding sow will be one that is purchased while it is a piglet. At this age, its quality cannot be fully assessed because pigs, like all other animals, can change dramatically as they mature. A young proven sow (one that has had one or more litters) of quality will obviously be very expensive. Thus, the breeder will need to balance age against numerous other factors.

PEDIGREE AND REGISTRATION

It is very important that your pet piggy comes with a pedigree and registration papers. They may be vital in your pet's being accepted as a pet potbelly by your local authority. More importantly, they confirm to you that your new pet is a genuine potbelly. A pedigree is no guarantee of quality, merely an indication of your pig's line of descent. The registration papers tell you that an association has checked the pedigree and verifies that the ancestors were potbellies and were registered with their association.

The breeding lines of these pets are very limited. All genuine potbellies will be traceable back to one of the two main breeding lines. They are those known as the Con line and the Lea line, which are named for their originators: Keith Connell (in Canada) and Keith Leavitt (in Texas). There are, of course, other established breeding lines today, but they will trace back to the founding stocks mentioned,

If you are not sure that a pig is a potbelly, ask to see the parents. If they are not available, ask to see pictures of them, or ask for a referral that may give a testimonial.

or, in more recent lines, to leading British, Swedish, and other European imports.

Sadly, there have been a number of reported cases of so-called brokers and breeders who sell pigs and have forged both pedigrees and registration papers. The only way you can be sure that you are not hoodwinked is to check the validity of these documents with the registration association concerned *before* you hand over any cash. Compare the registration description of the pig with what you see in front of you. Some breeders have crossed potbellies with regular farm pigs, and the offspring will likely grow to a size that is hardly miniature. Others may be selling other breeds of miniature pig as being potbellies. There is nothing wrong with any of the other established miniature pig breeds, but there is if they are sold as being potbellied pigs simply because potbellies command a better price or a more likely sale.

WHERE TO PURCHASE

You can save yourself a great deal of worry, such as that arising from the situation just discussed, by making sure you purchase your pet from a reputable source. Let us look at the market position from a very realistic standpoint. There are four basic sales outlets: One is the pet shop, the second is the broker, the third is the breeder, and the fourth is the animal shelter.

1. The pet shop. Pet shops purchase animals and resell them at a profit, thus providing a needed service to the public. However, some dealers and shops are more honest than others. Some have little knowledge at all about the care and problems of these pigs, which are still the new pet on the block. If you do decide to purchase from a dealer, be

very sure he is well established, meets all the criteria with regard to pig care, and can answer all of your questions about vaccinations, registration, pig ailments, training, and so on. If he cannot, then you will not get any backup service, which is most important.

2. The broker. Such a person could be a breeder who is acting for you because he himself does not have any piglets at the present time. It could also be a knowledgeable person who runs a genuine business bringing seller and buyers together for a fee. It could also be a person who has spotted a quick way to make some easy money preying on unsuspecting pet owners.

Genuine brokers will be quite happy to let you know the name of the breeder of the pigs being offered to you. Their fee will have been agreed upon with the breeder beforehand, and their role is purely to make the contact between the two parties. Thereafter, you can deal directly with the breeder if any problems arise. There are very few genuine brokers in the pet pig business at this time, though their numbers are likely to increase as the market expands. A less-than-honest broker will not let you know from whom the pig is coming and will probably operate from a temporary address. Excuses will be made as to why documentation cannot be given to you at time of purchase. I would be very careful indeed in purchasing a pet from a so-called broker.

When selecting a pig, choose one that is in sound condition. The health of a pet is more important than color or a bargain price tag.

3. The breeder. If you are seeking a particular color variety of potbelly that is widely unavailable, you can go to a breeder. However, not every breeder is actually honest, especially knowledgeable about pigs, or interested in your problems once he has your cash. There are a number of people who have jumped on the bandwagon simply to make money—a situation found with all other pets. Don't get me wrong; there is nothing wrong with a person commencing the

breeding of these pets with the intention of making a living from doing so. Many people do because it enables them to devote all their time to something they love and derive a living from it. Such breeders believe that after-sales service is vital. They also want to sell you pets they know will please you and be a credit to them. This is how it should be.

How do you decide who is and is not a good breeder to whom to hand over your hard-earned cash? The best way to find out is to visit breeders in their homes. You can then see their stock and the conditions under which they are living. This will tell you a great deal about how caring they are. If the conditions are dirty and the pigs are living in cramped accommodations, you can assume the breeder is essentially in potbellies simply to make money and has no regard for his animals.

As your priorities are health and pet potential, the piglets being offered should be in superb condition. They should be clean, lively, and very social. The breeder should be delighted to discuss any aspect of care with you. When he cannot answer a query, he will honestly tell you so. He will have all of the pedigrees and registration papers for his stock and will be happy to discuss them and other aspects of his program with you. He will almost certainly have one or more house-pet potbellies that will attest to how well they are cared for. Equally important, he will willingly supply you with the names and addresses of people to whom he has sold pets in the past—so you can check out the validity of his honesty. Chances are he will also ask you a lot of questions to determine if you are a suitable owner for his stock. Good breeders' love and concern for their pets is readily apparent. If you are left with any doubt about the honesty of a breeder, then it is best to look elsewhere. Such feelings usually stem from a genuine cause.

If breeders are not in your locality and you must purchase without

When seeking a potbelly, check more than one source, if possible, so that you may compare pigs and be able to choose the one most suitable for your wants and needs.

being able to visit their establishment, do take extra care to check out the standing of the person(s). You will see advertisements of the more established breeders in *POT-BELLIED PIGS* magazine, and you can contact any of the registration associations or clubs in order to make inquiries about them. Ask such associations if they can recommend specific breeders, rather than simply supply lists. Visit a potbelly show, and there you will meet numerous breeders who are keen enough that they want to show their little prides and joys. If you go about the selection process carefully and do not rush to buy from the first source, the chances are you will be delighted with your piglet and with the person who sells it to you.

Irrespective of the source of your pet, you should get certain written guarantees. You need to know that in the event that your pig is adjudged to have a health problem after being examined by a vet of your choice within 24 hours of your receiving the piglet, you will be entitled to return the pet and receive a full refund. The piglet should also come with a health certificate issued within 48 hours of its dispatch to you—and, of course, any other paperwork that might be involved in its transportation from the seller to your home.

If your piglet becomes ill some days after it was given a clean bill of health, you cannot fairly lay this on the seller because it may be that you have failed to provide the needed care. The first few weeks are always the most difficult when relocating a baby pig, which is why breeder after-sales service is so important.

4. Animal shelters. Apart from the regular animal shelter that takes in all kinds of pets, there are now several potbellied pig sanctuaries that cater only to displaced and abandoned piggies. While you might be able to obtain a potbelly at a very modest price from a regular shelter, you should bear in mind that it

Pigs are not dirty animals as most people believe. They like to have their surroundings and bedding clean.

Piglets are adorable; selecting one out of this group would surely be difficult.

probably arrived there due to a problem. It may be aggressive or totally untrained in a home environment. Such pigs will need very special understanding and skillful retraining, so they may not be at all suited to your particular needs.

Those obtained via a potbelly sanctuary will be a better bet because the staff of such an establishment will be knowledgeable about pigs. They will advise you on the suitability of any piggies that they have to your particular needs and level of animal experience.

THE COST OF A POTBELLY

You will normally get what you pay for when you purchase any animal species as a pet. At this time, potbellied pigs exchange hands for as little as $100 and upwards for a pet to as much as $25,000 for a high-quality breeding boar or sow. The only way you can establish what a current fair price should be is by contacting a number of breeders and telling them exactly what you are looking for. In some instances, the breeder will quote you the basic price of the pet, to which must be added the cost of neutering, vaccinations, and health certificate. Others will quote an inclusive price, to which the costs for transportation and documentation must be added if the pet is to be sent across state lines.

Do take into account that a housetrained and well-socialized pet will normally be more costly than one that is simply a straight-from-the-breeding-pen pet. The extra cost of the trained and socialized pig is normally a very sound investment and means you will experience far less problems from the outset. The non-black pigs are currently very popular so they tend to be more costly. This does not make them superior as pets; it merely reflects the supply and demand situation. If color is not a major factor to you, then a good black pig represents excellent value.

In general, you will not find bargains in pet species. However, the potbellied pig market is new and expanding rapidly. This situation brings with it a number of problems for genuine breeders. A number of backyard breeders are resorting to almost intensive farming methods in order to generate as many piglets as they can. They undersell the genuine breeder. The reality is then that no matter how good a breeder's pigs are, he may be forced to drastically discount his price if he has a need to sell surplus stock.

Many leading breeders are having to rethink their selling strategies because the initial high prices they could obtain for pets is being undercut by the large number of backyard breeders.

The answer is that the genuine breeder must carefully regulate his output to match the available market. I mention these facts because they do mean that at this time and for a few years into the future, the potbelly pig market will be in a state of flux. Bargains are to be had, but deciding what is a bargain piglet and what is just a cheap backyard pig of poor potential can only be determined if you take the time to carefully research the standing of the seller.

Do not let price alone be the major factor in determining from whom you will purchase. Your greatest concern is that your pet must come from a breeder who truly cares for his pigs and has a proven track record of following up his sales with service. You do not need to pay an excessive price to obtain a delightful pet, but you should be prepared to pay a price that reflects the cost and time the breeder has put into the piglet in order to ensure that it will make the transition from his home to yours as problem free as possible.

With regard to selecting a healthy pig, you should trust in the honesty of the seller. This assumes that your

Selecting a quality potbelly will require that you do some homework. Acquire as much information on what a sound and healthy pig should look like before you begin your search.

Reputable breeders will be able to guarantee that their pigs are purebred potbellies by providing pedigree information. They will also be available to answer any care and training questions after the purchase.

selection process has been sound. This said, you should be aware of the basic conformation of a potbelly and how you can ascertain if it is healthy. Again, if you view enough actual pigs, as well as photos of sound specimens, it is far less likely that you will be sold an inferior potbelly. A final comment with regard to a pet piglet is this: if the owner cannot lift the piglet up to show it to you without it squealing at the top of its voice, it has not been socialized very well. You will need to spend a great deal of time doing what a good breeder would have done in the first place.

The Standard and the Colors

In order for anything to be assessed, there must be some yardstick against which its quality can be judged. In animals, this is a written standard of excellence. Such a standard may be applicable throughout an entire country if a single national organization exists. Where two or more national organizations are in operation, the standard will apply only within the organization that drafts it. The latter situation occurs with numerous pet animals, and this is the case with potbellied pigs. In this book, the standard quoted is that of the National Committees On Potbellied Pigs (NCOPP) and is reproduced with their kind permission.

The majority of pet owners will not be unduly concerned with the standard, though its thoughtful application will ultimately affect the quality of the pets that are made available. However, if you plan to involve yourself in breeding or exhibition, the standard will have a profound effect upon your future success. The exhibition side of potbellies will grow at a rapid rate, and it will become the determining factor as to how the hobby will expand. The standard is thus worthy of special consideration at this juncture in the development of these pets.

INTERPRETATION OF STANDARDS

Before quoting the standard for a potbelly pig, it is worthwhile to draw your attention to certain aspects that are applicable to any animal standard. The first point is that no standard is ever so specific that it is inflexible. It would, in fact, be impossible to draft an exact standard simply because no two pigs can ever be quite the same. Initially, all standards tend to be more flexible when they are drafted than might be the case as the years roll by.

A standard is open to varying interpretations and is essentially a consensus of opinions based on the views of those chosen to form a standards committee. If it is found that the standard, perhaps through being too loose in its terminology, is being interpreted in a way that is considered detrimental to the hobby (which does not always mean to the animal itself), it is then revised to overcome any problems that have become apparent. A standard is thus not an immutable text, nor should it ever be so.

When you read the following standard, it probably fits your pig exactly—or nearly so in your eyes. However, this also applies to just about every other pet potbelly in your country. A standard can therefore only be fully appreciated after you have read it and compared its wording against very many potbellied pigs. The subtle differences between good and bad then become more and more obvious. At this point in time, the gene pool in potbellies is very limited if compared to most other popular pets. This means that the overall standard of quality in potbellies is relatively consistent. As the hobby expands, the differences between what is perceived as quality, mediocrity, and pure rubbish will

When purchasing a pig for show or breeding purposes, a greater knowledge of the written standard is essential than when purchasing a household pet.

become much more apparent. It is the wording of the standard and its interpretation by judges that will influence how breeders select their stock. It will create what are known as fashions, which are, to a degree, inevitable because of the very flexibility and limited wordage of the standard.

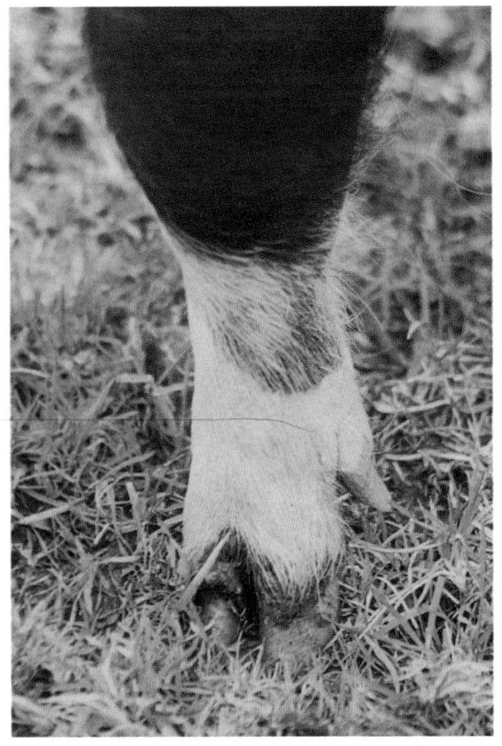

The condition of the legs and feet is very important to the well-being of the pig. Short, strong legs with tight, well-rounded feet are needed to adequately carry around these bulky little animals.

LIMITATIONS OF A STANDARD

The vast majority of standards used for exhibition animals rarely takes any account of either the breeding worth or the disposition of the animal. This is so in potbellies, in which disposition accounts for only 5 of the 100 points allocated to the pig. Breeding worth is relative to the standard only inasmuch as a pig that meets the standard is more likely to pass on at least some virtues than a pig that has no virtues to start with! A standard is thus limited in certain aspects of assessing quality.

Its role is essentially to enable people to distinguish good from bad based purely on external appearance. When selecting a sow for future breeding, and more so when evaluating a boar, it is most important that a potential breeder does not get carried away solely by the external appearance and show-winning record of the animal.

It must always be remembered that a top show-winner may have received its beautiful conformation as much by pure chance as by its breeding. In such instances, it is unlikely that all, or even most, of its virtues will be passed on to its offspring. A less impressive-looking pig that has been carefully bred may win few prizes yet be capable of producing offspring of a much higher and consistent standard than a top winner. Such a potbelly is thus a much better investment if it is to be part of a breeding program.

THE NCOPP STANDARD FOR POTBELLIED PIGS (TOTAL OF 100 POINTS)

1. General appearance—40 Points

Attractive individuality with (femininity, masculinity) vigor, harmonious blending at all parts, and impressive style and carriage. All parts of the potbellied pig should be considered in evaluating their general appearance, especially the pronounced potbellied swayed back, erect ears and straight tail.

Breed Characteristics—10 Points

Head: Proportionate to body. Neat in appearance.

Bite: Not overshot or undershot. (Severe cases of overshot or undershot are severe defects.)

Eyes: Eyes should be clear, bright,

This 5 month old piglet displays quality characteristics, such as the gently swayed back, small, straight ears and strong, straight legs, to name a few.

deep set, and not bulging.

Face: Medium width in combination of eyes, snout, and ears. (A long exaggerated face is undesirable.)

Nose: Short to medium in length, proportionate to head.

Allowance for free passage of air when breathing normally.

Jowls: Medium to full is acceptable, yet not overfat.

Ears: Small, erect, somewhat flat.

Potbellied Characteristic—10 Points

Exaggerated belly; however, the belly should not be bulging to a degree that it hangs or drags on the ground. The belly will develop as animals mature in all genders. Viewing from the top of the animal, the belly should not protrude from the side (except pregnant females).

Back and Tail—10 Points

Back: Gently swayed, yet not exaggerated. The sway should be in proportion to the length of the back. A “cubby” pig is shorter in length and more desirable but must also be in proportion to overall view of the pig.

Tail: Straight. Attaches high on the rump.

Size—10 Points

Maximum acceptable height (at 1 year of age) is 18 in. at point of shoulder. Ideal height is 14 in. or less at point of shoulder.

2. Body—35 Points

Front end (neck, withers, chest, and shoulders)—10 Points

Neck: Reasonably short, blending smoothly into jowls and shoulders.

Withers: Level and smooth, tying into shoulder smoothly.

Chest: Medium width (not wide or

narrow).

Shoulder: Even and smooth. No more than 1 in. lower than the hipbone. Full, not angular sloping from side to side.

Back, Rump and Hips—10 Points

Back: Gently swayed, yet not exaggerated.

Rump: Full and level, flowing gently to the base of the tail.

(Rounded or angular rump with a low-hung tail is undesirable.)

Hips: Wide, pleasingly rounded. Hips should be no higher than 1 in. above the point of shoulder. Level is most desirable.

Legs and Feet—15 Points

Strong bones, pasterns short and strong, hocks cleanly molded.

Feet: Short, compact and well rounded, with deep heel and level sole.

Forelegs: Short in length, straight, medium width between and squarely placed.

Hindlegs: Nearly perpendicular from hock to pastern, from side view, and straight from the rear view.

3. Reproductive system—10 Points

Teats: Evenly spaced, 5 on each side. Especially important for boars and gilts. Not vital for altered-sex animals.

Vulva: Not too small or too large.

Testicles: Boars should have visible testicles.

4. Movement—7 Points

Stride should be smooth and free in movement. Front and rear legs should move out freely. There should be no stiff gait or limping.

5. Disposition—5 Points

A friendly disposition is highly desirable in all genders.

6. Skin and hair—3 Points

Skin should be supple and be in good condition. Hair, all lengths acceptable as long as the animal is healthy and shows no signs of worms or malnutrition.

A potbelly's tail is straight as is shown here, but it should be set higher on the rump.

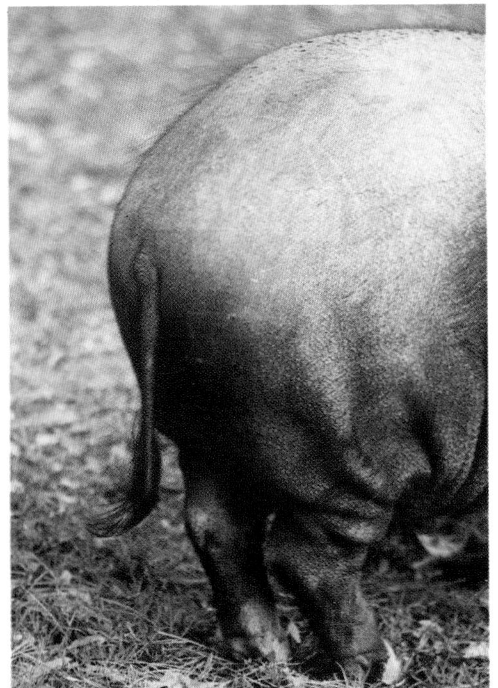

COLOR STANDARDS

These standards are strictly color definitions, whose purpose is to be descriptive. They are not to suggest or imply that one color or pattern is better than another.

Black: Solid black with no other marking of any other sort on any part of the body including the leather on the snout.

Black/white markings: Any white markings on black which include, but are not limited to, socks, stockings, stars, blazes, white tip tail, white tufts on the head, snout markings, white belly, and white collar (partial, half, or full).

Collar pig: Must have a full color that does not connect to the belly.

Pinto: The ground color of the body should be white with a "black saddle" which does not intermingle

There is no preferred color in pig standards. This specimen exhibits the fancy pinto markings. Notice the halo around the saddle pattern.

with itself except at the back legs. The black saddle may include the head of the pig and extend the length of the body or less. Other black markings are acceptable as in black spot on belly, black head, etc. The face can include white markings that include, but are not limited to, stars, blazes, white tufts on the head, etc. The pinto may or may not have a white collar.

Fancy pinto: Same as pinto. However, the saddle has a halo. A halo is where the hair overlaps the skin color. For example, white hair laying over black skin. The saddle does not intermingle with itself, and the saddle edges must be seen from the side and rear view of the pig.

Smooth saddles fancy pinto: Same as fancy pinto. However, the halo width of the saddle is consistent around the edges of the saddle.

White: Solid white hair with pink skin and no other markings of any sort on any part of the body including a pink leather snout.

White/black markings: Any black patch skin pigment markings on white which include, but are not limited to, behind the ears, snout markings, on the head, jowls, throat, withers, rump, etc.

Pebble: Solid white pig with gray, silver, or black “pebble spots” located, but not limited to, behind the ears, on the head, jowls, throat, withers or entire body.

Silver: Solid silver pig with no other markings. Colors can vary from champagne silver, gray silver, blue silver, ash silver, etc.

Silver pinto: The ground color of the body should be ivory with a “silver saddle” that does not intermingle with itself except at the back legs. The silver saddle may include the head of the pig and extend the length of the body or less. Other black markings are acceptable

These white colored piglets show signs of good health. Notice the smooth, clean skin and hair. Proper care, as well as good breeding, is important in maintaining healthy looking pigs.

as in silver spot on belly, silver head, etc.

The face can include ivory markings that include, but are not limited to, stars, blazes, white tufts on the head, snout markings, etc.

Fancy silver pinto: Same as silver pinto. However, the saddle has a halo. A halo is where the hair overhangs the skin color. For example, silver hair laying over black skin. The saddle does not intermingle with itself, and the saddle edges must be seen from the side and rear view of the pig.

Any other variety: Includes any other color variety. Eye color is not a factor in determining color descriptions.

COMMENTS ON THE STANDARD

The worth of any standard is based not only on what it states but also on what it does not. Further, any features that are regarded as being unacceptable should be made very apparent within the standard. We all have an opinion on what we feel is needed in the standards of the pets that we keep. These opinions provide for healthy discussion. If we are to use the standard as a criterion of what should and should not be, it is only right that fair comment on it should be applied by those bound by it. With this in mind, I venture a few comments.

The most obvious omission from the present standard is that it features neither disqualifications nor faults that should preclude an exhibit from gaining championship status or even a first prize. For example, it states that "severe cases of overshot or undershot are severe faults." Given that such features are genetically controlled, will affect the snout length and appearance, and a pig's ability to eat correctly, it would seem to me that they deserve greater attention than merely being a parenthetical addition under "Bite." They should merit disqualification, which makes it quite clear to a breeder that dentition is a very important feature. Continuing with the subject of dentition, the standard states that which is not required, rather than what is, which is what a standard should do. Is the preferred bite a scissor (the upper incisor teeth overlapping but just touching the lower teeth) or pincer (the incisor teeth of upper and lower jaws meeting together), or is either of them equally acceptable? Further, like most other animal standards, that of the potbelly makes no distinction between juveniles and adults in respect to the teeth. Assessment of dentition, in other than very bad cases, can only be made once a pig is mature because the jaws do not grow proportionately. They can change with maturity. In some dog and cat breeds, the teeth are often ignored by judges and breeders alike. Were this not the case, certain breeds simply could not exist. The health, vigor, and temperament of a pet are probably its most important features. Teeth should be a priority in potbellies if the hobby is not to slide in the same way as have these other two pets. It would be nice to see the desired dental formula of the pig quoted in the standard, as well as the digital formula.

While stating that the tail should be straight, the importance of this feature is such that I would have included a kinked or curly tail as being a major disqualifying fault. Likewise, in the case of boars, the lack of two descended testicles should merit disqualification—not simply loss of a few points as is implied in the present standard.

The term "proportionate" is always a difficult word to explain. While accepting that its use can never be adequately related in words, I do think there are instances where it can be qualified in such a way as to place limits on what is and is not acceptable. This is especially useful where there is likely to be an undesirable change in a feature's proportions, based either on what the standard already calls for or on what has happened with other popular pets.

The standard clearly favors a movement toward smaller pigs. At the same time it also states that "A cubby pig is shorter in length and more

Not only is conformation important in the potbelly, disposition is also considered when breeding. Gentle and kind natures make for better companions.

desirable." It does not actually state that there is any relationship between the length of the pig and its height—thus the length of its legs. However, I think most breeders would accept that some limits should be set if the breed is not to develop an excess of back, as has been seen in some horses and dog breeds, or the opposite situation. To a degree, the potbelly will limit back length and height ratios, but not an unduly short back.

Unless guidelines are in place, breeders and judges just might interpret the standard in a variety of ways. Given that this is a distinct possibility, could not the standard relate a proportion of back length to shoulder height? For example, in German Shepherd Dog standards, the ratio is as 10 is to $8\frac{1}{2}$ or 9. Such a guideline, worked out to the established proportions in the potbelly pig, would mean that regardless of whether the breed gets smaller it would not lose its adjudged desirable proportions.

The present standard calls for five pairs of teats in each sex but does not indicate that there may be six pairs, which is the normal number for all domestic variants of the genus *Sus*.

You will note that in the potbelly, unlike in most other pets, color plays no part in evaluating a quality pig. If a prediction was to be made with regard to the standard, it would be that color will account for points at some future date as the color-breeding side of the hobby becomes more established. Color points could easily replace those presently given to reproductive aspects, which could form part of the disqualification or the withholding of first-prize faults.

One aspect of the standard, which is not an omission but an interesting consideration, is the following: the present standard, like that in most, though not all, other pets, makes no allowance for intangible qualities. This point is perhaps best illustrated

Some pigs have hardly any hair at all, while others will exhibit greater amounts. This pig has longer hair, creating a mane like appearance that extends down the ridge of the back.

Conditioning pigs at an early age to be trusting of people is very important. Unsocialized pigs will be difficult, cautious, and harder to train as they get older

by the phrase "the whole is better than the sum of the individual parts." A beautiful potbelly is not a collection of individual parts per se but a collection of parts that is intrinsically put together in very subtle proportions so that the finished image is one of great beauty.

The importance of this idea can easily be seen in the following example. Most standards work on the basic premise that an exhibit starts with 100 points and then loses points for its shortcomings. A judge thus has no latitude to give points for an especially outstanding virtue—other than to give it the maximum number of points allocated to that feature. However, this alone may not be sufficient.

If a given pig has few faults, it will lose few points, yet it may not have that special something that makes it stand out from the average winner. Another pig may lose more points on a piece-by-piece basis yet possess an indefinable excellence. This excellence could be labeled imposing appearance, elegance, or quality and might actually class the animal, in spite of its shortcomings, as a superior potbelly, compared to the one that was difficult to fault—but equally difficult in which to find outstanding merit.

The standard is thus not simply a collection of words that describe what a good potbelly should look like but is a blueprint of the breed and actually embodies within it a whole philosophy. On the interpretation of this philosophy rests the total credibility and the future-development direction of the entire hobby. If you become a breeder/exhibitor, do take an active interest in the standard—and all that it implies—of your chosen registration body. It is the source of some really healthy club discussions, as this text has shown. It is from such debates that your ruling association will no doubt welcome input.

Preparing for Your Piglet

In many ways, the arrival of a little piglet into a home can be compared with the arrival of a baby. Indeed, most piggy owners will tell you that caring for a potbellied pig is very comparable in nearly all respects to caring for a child. Piglets are very sensitive to changes in temperature so they must always be kept warm.

In spite of their reputation as gluttons, little piglets do have very delicate stomachs that can easily be upset if their diet is less than correct.

All of this means that you should prepare for your new pet in advance of its arrival. Because it will need a lot of comforting as it changes homes, its arrival should take place when you have more than normal time to devote to it, e.g., when you have a few days off from work or on a weekend. This works both ways because it is a very exciting time for the whole family. While you can obtain your new companion at any time of the year, it would make sense to become a proud new owner during the spring through summer period. At that time of year, the weather is nice; and porky can be allowed out of doors for his exercise and in order to play in your garden.

BASIC CONSIDERATIONS

The first comment I would make with respect to porcine housing is that I do not consider that a pig is a pet suited to apartment life. Not every owner would agree with this statement, but it is based on very sound management principles and realities. In an apartment, it is quite impossible to provide the kind of facility that a pig should have at its disposal. Of course, a case could be made for the suitability of almost any other animal to an apartment, it being a question of how much one wishes to consider the animal's natural needs as opposed to the mere provision of a life-sustaining environment. Pigs can be kept for their entire life in a small pigpen, but this does not make a pigpen a suitable home or make the pigs well-balanced pets.

Successful pet ownership is based on having a situation in which the potential problems are reduced to a minimum. This in turn greatly reduces the chances that the animal will be neglected or will display a personality problem as a direct result of its environment. Many potbelly owners who have purchased these pets and have tried to care for them in restricted environments have found difficulties that would not have arisen had a yard or garden been part of their home. The vast majority of pigs that end up in animal shelters will come from urban situations, and, in particular, from homes that have no outdoor facilities for them.

Pigs like to root, and they like to browse on foliage. They also like to be able to exercise gently, and they enjoy the wind, sun, and even rain as much as we do. They like to wallow in water on hot days. To

This quality blue-eyed pinto boar is enjoying a nice sunny day about the yard.

suggest that they do not miss what they have never known is akin to saying that a tiger that has always been kept in a large cage will not be affected by such a confined existence. A pet pig that has daily access to the outside world will be a contented pet that will be very happy to live in a house. It will be less grumpy and less moody.

It is true that an apartment-dwelling pig can be taken out every day in order to exercise, and a rooting facility can be provided within a home. However, in many instances, such confined pets are not taken out as often as they should be: either the weather is not good or the owner has to go somewhere. There is always a reason why the pet cannot be taken out on a given day. This results in a moody pig and, ultimately, in a dissatisfied owner. The situation then steadily deteriorates to the point that piggy becomes an unwanted pet. I do not say this is the way it has to be, but it is a typical scenario in many instances. We are talking about the average first-time potbelly owner, not the small group of owners who are prepared to go to whatever lengths are needed to ensure that their pets are given the kind of care required to overcome confining accommodations.

Ideal accommodations are those in which a yard is part of the home and where a small area can be fenced in to create a piggy pound. This may simply be an outdoor exercise area, or it may be the site of an outdoor potbelly house. The larger the exercise area the better, because this will result in minimal damage to the soil and to whatever vegetation is growing. The area should be fenced in a secure manner so that porky cannot get out and so that stray dogs or coyotes (depending on where you live) cannot get in.

If the outdoor area is a planted garden, do bear in mind that your pet will delight in rooting around in any loose soil. This means that it will disturb and probably devour any flowering plants. Needless to say, it will uproot and gobble vegetables with great delight. If your garden is unfenced, you must rectify this situation. It will certainly be a local-ordinance requirement, but also it will prevent your pet from trotting off around the neighborhood and having a feast at the expense of other residents' prize plants.

If you are to provide outdoor accommodations for porky, they must be solid and very draftproof. While a large kennel-type structure would be acceptable, it is altogether better that the home be tall enough so that you can enter

In confined areas, clean shredded paper will make good ground covering and bedding.

without having to stoop. This will make general cleaning chores much easier to attend to. It would also be preferable that the accommodations are equipped with utilities such as electricity, water, and sewerage. If you live in an area that experiences either very hot, and, more especially, very cold seasons, electricity will be invaluable in order to provide heating during the cold months and ventilation—via fans—during the summer.

Of course, the outdoor housing might only be utilized for limited periods because your pet, if it is to be just that, will no doubt be living in your home most of the time. If a pet pig is housed outdoors for long periods, it will never develop into the type of intimate pet that it would have had it lived with you. The whole idea of an outdoor facility for a house pet is to provide a place in which it can root around, relax, and generally enjoy itself on those nice spring, summer, and autumn days. It should never be a place to which your pet is banished and ignored because you have encountered a problem with the animal.

If you plan to breed potbellies, then you should devote considerably more thought to the question of housing. You will need it to be more extensive and substantial, so that it also provides work areas and storage areas. In all instances, you will require a solid floor—probably of concrete—for the outdoor home. It should have a very slight slope to it so that when it is hosed, the water will easily run off to a disposal point. Alternatively, if it is flat, you should incorporate a concrete gully that the water can be brushed/ hosed into and thus carried to a drainage point.

The floor should be covered with a very generous bed of either straw or wood shavings, or a bed of shavings with a pile of straw and hay in one corner, where piggy can

The importance of a confined outside area for your pig cannot be stressed enough. Here it will satisfy its natural urge to root, as well as enjoy the weather and fresh air.

A pig in a blanket—A nap among pillows, blankets, and a favorite toy seem to be at the top of the list for all piggies.

fashion a cozy nest in which to sleep. Such a nest will also have the advantage that if porky gets muddy, he will clean himself very well in the bedding. Avoid the use of cedar wood shavings as they are regarded as being somewhat toxic—pine is the better choice. You might feature a good-sized sleeping box in which the straw is retained by side and back panels. However, be sure that such a box is very low to the ground so that your pet can walk into it with no difficulty. Little piglets are quite nimble, but this changes as they mature.

If space permits, it is useful to have a concrete yard just outside of the porcine house and which allows entry into the pasture area. This will restrict the amount of mud you will have to wade through during rainy weather, which will be the case if the soil area abuts the pet's home. Always bear in mind the golden rule that the more convenient it is for you to attend to needs in and around your pet's home, the less the jobs become chores that you might thus neglect.

In the summer, provide a wading pool for your pig. It will be essential in keeping it cool. A pig can be badly affected by the heat and can easily suffer from heat stroke.

One facility that all pet pigs should be provided with is that of a wading pool. Like us humans, pigs suffer badly when it is very hot. Such a pool might be temporary, in the form of a child's wading pool (with a reinforced base so that your pet's hooves do not tear it), or it might be a permanent feature of the accommodations. Constructing a pool is not that difficult. You can make one from a variety of materials including concrete, fiber glass, or even one of the strong butyl rubbers used in the construction of a garden pond.

The pool should have a gentle slope so that porky can enter or exit from it without any problems. The base should then be flat. The depth can be anything from 15cm (6 in.) to 31cm (12 in.); somewhere between these extremes is probably best for the average potbelly. If you have two or more pigs, it would be more practical if the pool was fitted with a bottom drain to make cleaning easier—but this could alternatively be effected with a small diaphragm pump connected to a hose.

The pool should be large enough so that your pet can easily turn around. There are now a number of commercially-made wading pools produced for potbellies (available from specialty piggy dealers).

Your pig's house should be light and airy, with windows that can be opened during warm weather. However, the actual pen(s) should be arranged so that your pet can always move into a shady area. A split barnyard door is another useful feature of a piggy home. Ventilation should be provided by vents that are situated both low down and high up in the living quarters—the air should circulate

This piglet wants to join in the wading activities. A child's wading pool will not stand up to pigs' hooves; a sturdier set up will last longer.

freely.

Many potbelly owners have constructed quite luxurious homes for their pets, some complete with central heating, air conditioning, closed-circuit TV, and even background music!

It is a sad reflection on our society that I should have to add that if your pets are to live in outdoor accommodations, it is essential that they be very secure. Unfortunately, there are those who may attempt to steal your pets as an easy way of making money. This sad situation is seen with koi (colored carp), dogs, cats, and exotic aviary birds. Apart from the loss of investment, it is more a case of the worry and unhappiness that result for the owners. Situate outdoor housing in good sight of your home, the nearer the better. Fit strong padlocks and, if you can afford it, an alarm system. In any event, always feature a nightlight in your arrangement as it will inhibit many from attempting to enter your property. Of course, it is also wise to have the ear of your pet tattooed with your registration number or another mark of identification. Microchip implants can also be used and the details recorded with your registry service.

INDOOR ACCOMMODATIONS

The requirements for housing a piglet indoors are obviously far less than for outdoors because temperature and weather protection are normally not factors with which to be contended. Nonetheless, advance planning for the arrival of your porcine pet is important for a number of reasons. Where it will sleep, what rooms it will be allowed in, and how it can be confined when necessary are all questions that must be addressed.

Initially, and until it is fully housetrained, it will be best to restrict your piggie's freedom to one, at best two, of your rooms. This will prevent a lot of toiletry accidents on your carpet.

You are advised to purchase, or make, a reasonably-sized pen and situate it in a convenient location in the kitchen or utility room—where porky can see you most of the time yet where the pen is not in your way. The size of the pen will obviously reflect that of the piglet and should allow for growth. As long as it provides room for your pet to turn around in, and to house its feeding utensils and litterbox, it will be large enough. It should have a sturdy floor and a small edging around it so that bedding, should it be shavings, is retained in the pen.

Playpens for human babies, or those for puppies, can be obtained commercially. Alternatively, you can make your own using sturdy wire mesh and wood. A playpen is invariably a square, but this need not be so if your kitchen or living room configuration would better accommodate a longer but narrower pen. A piggy pen is not an essential item, but its value is in ensuring that porky can be housetrained much easier than if he has unrestricted freedom. There will always be times when you wish you could confine your pet, and it is a good part of the pet's general training.

An alternate means of confining a piglet is to purchase a crate or pet carrier: the kind that is used for dogs and cats. Such a unit makes an ideal place for your piglet to sleep in during its early days in your home. It is also an indispensable means of transporting your piggy to the vet or elsewhere while he is small. You can purchase these units in a range of sizes. One that is on the large side will give you longer wear than one that is smaller and perhaps more ideal to start with but that will soon be outgrown. All

A crate is especially beneficial in keeping a young piglet confined, when not under supervision, until it knows the rules of the home. It also offers a secure place for it to sleep in the evening or to nap in during the day.

pig owners should possess a crate or pet carrier of one type or another.

The sleeping arrangements that you choose will naturally reflect your views on just how personal your pet will become. In other words, you may decide to confine porky to the kitchen or another room, you might place him in a pen or crate, or you might allow him to share your own bed. The last opinion just mentioned is the choice for many pet potbelly owners as long as the piggy is housetrained.

Although they make great household pets, it is extremely important for potbellies to have an outside area in which they can exercise, play, and root. If an adequate outside environment is not provided, it may result in unhappy, destructive pets.

Potbellies make remarkably fine feet warmers or hot water bottles; but if the piglet is allowed to share your bed, do bear in mind that it would be unfair to later change this rule as he gets larger and heavier.

Getting onto your bed is, of course, not an easy matter for a pig. While it is small, you can easily lift it up, but as it grows you might need to supply a piggy ramp or other aids, depending on the height of your bed.

A very popular choice of bedding for pet pigs is a large beanbag, which enables your pet to fashion a really comfortable spot on it. Another suitable bed would be a large, but very low, wooden dog bed that is amply supplied with blankets and cushions.

Yet another method some owners have found successful is to place a sleeping bag on top of blankets. Porky will soon work out how to snuggle into the bag! Be sure, however, that the chosen bag is easily washed. If you are looking for something more special for your pet, then how about a low pig-sized bed that can be placed next to yours, complete with pillows and blankets?

Note the stress on warm bedding. Even in a warm room, you would still ensure that a human infant was protected from drafts, and you would supply extra overnight bedding clothes if your central heating was lowered to a lower temperature. Regard your piglet as you would a human baby, and later as you would yourself. This means that if you feel chilled or hot, so will your pet—potbellies really are just like us in their temperature preferences.

A favorite pastime for pigs is eating. Proper feed dishes should be heavy, low lipped, and wide.

FEEDING UTENSILS

You will need a food bowl and a water bowl. It is strongly recommended that you also provide a rooting box. Pigs, of course, have rather large jowls so the food bowl should be large and low lipped. It can be made of crock or metal. Pet shops stock dishes that are suitable for pigs.

The drawback with any dish that is lightweight is that it will be pushed around the floor and may also be flung about like a toy. This is much less likely with a large solid-crock dog bowl, which initially may be rather tall for a little piglet.

Pigs in the wild obtain most of their food by foraging, or rooting up, the earth. You can provide the means of their being able to do this in your home by making them a rooting box. This is best made of wood, with sides and a back that are a few inches tall to retain the contents but with a very low front so that your piggy has no problems walking in and out. Make the box large enough so that your pet can turn around in it.

The box is then filled with an assortment of large- and medium-sized pebbles and stones. Among them can be scattered various food items. Porky will devote a great deal of time foraging in the box for part of his daily rations. This enables him to fulfill a natural desire to root around; and thus it helps him towards psychological contentment, an important aspect of his life.

PIGGY TOYS

Baby pigs will amuse themselves with a whole range of toys, but do be sure that they are not the kind that can easily be swallowed or that contain sharp metal strands. As with dogs and cats, it is actually the simplest things that amuse pigs of any age. For example, they love rummaging under sheets of newspaper, and a cardboard box filled with this material and open on one end will keep them happy for a long while. Unlike cats and dogs, which are predators and thus natural chasers of things, pigs are rummagers, and this should be reflected in what they are offered as toys. A pile of scatter or throw cushions is another very popular means of amusing porky. A low box filled with broken fruit branches is a variation on the rooting box and will also be quite fascinating to a pig. The large dog chews made of hide are yet another item that will keep porky occupied for quite some time.

GROOMING AIDS

Because it has very little hair, you will not need a comb for your piglet, but one or more brushes will be useful. You might see little point in grooming any creature that is almost bald, but you would be wrong. For one thing, grooming will help tone the skin of your pet. Further, the very action of grooming means that your pet will

A simple ball will keep your potbelly amused for hours; it will enjoy rolling it about with its nose.

become familiar with being touched on areas of its body that are sensitive. This is most important in your pig's socialization training. Any medium-bristle brush will be satisfactory, as will a rubber curry brush (as used on horses) that features a loop through which you can place your hand. Some brushes have rubber on one side and bristle on the other.

It is important that the hooves are cared for, and so you should obtain a suitable hoof conditioner. An emery board can be used to keep piggy's toenails in shape, but later on you may need horse hoof trimmers—or you may prefer to let your vet attend to keeping the nails to the correct length. There are numerous lotions that you can obtain in order to give the skin a polished look, but remember that true skin condition comes essentially from good nutrition—anything else is actually a surface polish and merely disguises that which may be lacking in the skin. Nonetheless, a mist-spray bottle will be useful to spray a glycerine-and-water mixture on porky. A weekly application will help to keep the skin moist and supple if the air in your home is on the dry side.

TRAINING AIDS

In order to be able to take your potbelly for walks, to the vet's, and on vacation (if porky is to go as well), it will be necessary that he is lead trained. Your pet will need a harness and a lead. These items come in three basic sizes (small, medium, and large) and can be purchased via mail order from piggy outfitters if your pet shop does not stock them.

There are two commonly seen styles of harness. One is a figure-eight conformation (the most popular); the other is two loops of material connected along the back by a third strand. The latter is popular with those who train their dogs to track. It is the one preferred by this author because it does not interfere at all with the gait of the wearer—and

Potbellied pigs make excellent companions for elderly people. They don't require rigorous exercise.

The most important part of porkys' schooling will be that of harness and lead training. This will give you the freedom of taking piggy out with you wherever you go.

thus is more comfortable. The important consideration with a harness is that it be neither too tight nor too loose. It should not chafe and create sores on any part of the pig's body. Nylon is the most used material because it is very flexible and light. Soft leather is also a good choice though it is not readily available. Obtain a harness made specifically for pigs because their conformation is obviously very different from that of a cat or a dog.

Leads come in various lengths, but one that is six feet or longer would be the most suitable. If you require an especially long lead, then contact a supplier of dog training equipment (maybe via your local dog-training club). Always select harnesses and leads that are up to the job. In particular, the harness ring that will take the lead should be strong, as should the lead-fastening clip. Billet hooks must be made of *substantial* steel, not the flimsy kind used on inexpensive leads—which can suddenly break open. Trigger hooks are usually very strong. Also, the harness and the lead should be sewn at the points that take the stress, not secured by inexpensive rivets. Fortunately, mature pigs, unlike dogs, are unlikely to take off at high speed if the lead snaps at a weak point. Even so, investment in the best equipment is always a prudent policy, and it will virtually last a lifetime.

OTHER CONSIDERATIONS

Before your new pet arrives, you must check that there are no dangers in your home. Examples would be trailing electrical wires that are plugged into sockets. Piglets love to nibble on things, and such wires are thus potentially lethal to them. Some houseplants may be toxic if eaten, apart from which you would not wish to see your cherished vegetation used as a meal by porky. Place them well out of reach. Fragile ornaments should likewise be placed where an inquisitive piglet cannot knock them over.

Be aware that pigs are amazingly clever when it comes to getting into cupboards—using their snouts almost like hands. Combine this fact with their passionate hobby of searching for food, and it adds up to a disruptive—and maybe dangerous—pastime. Pigs will happily chew on plastic bottles containing detergents and other chemicals. They will cover themselves in boot polish or other cleaning aids, and they will delight in dragging everything from a cupboard just to double check that some morsel has not been overlooked. The answer is to make sure that dangerous items are kept out of their reach and food cupboards securely locked.

The matter of slippery floors requires special consideration. If the rooms to which your pet is allowed access have slippery floors, it would be wise to invest in a few non-slip mats. They are especially useful on kitchen floors.

Baby piglets are not idiots; thus they are unlikely to hurl themselves from open balconies, or into swimming pools or garden ponds. This said, they do panic very quickly if startled. Under such conditions, they might accidentally fall. Such potential accidents must therefore be guarded against by taking the appropriate precautions, the best of which is to temporarily fence off dangerous areas.

If there are a few steps to climb from your garden to your home, it might be

Some people like to dress their pigs up for special occasions. This piggy seems to have learned to enjoy such pampering and attention.

Pigs are very curious creatures. Make sure any valuable or breakable items are out of porky's reach.

worthwhile to erect a ramp for porky's use. It can be made from wood and covered with indoor/outdoor carpet so that it provides a non-slip grip. Side railings to protect against falls would be wise. A piglet can climb steps well enough, but the more mature pet might appreciate a ramp. Breeders might find it worthwhile to invest in a commercially-made movable ramp or chute.

If you really do not want to permanently section off a part of your garden for piggy's play area, you can purchase collapsible wire panels that can be assembled into temporary pens. They are very useful if you plan to travel with your pig. Suppliers of all of the items suggested in this and other chapters do advertise in *POT-BELLIED PIGS* magazine, so you should have no difficulty in locating sources of equipment.

Finally, do not forget to have on hand about a two-week supply of food of the brand that the breeder has been using. Exactly how much you decide to store will obviously reflect how readily you can obtain the desired foods in your area. The more prepared you are in advance for the arrival of your piggy, the less problems you should encounter.

Porcine Nutrition

The feeding of any animal species is not an exact science, though it can appear so if you read the extensive literature that is produced by food manufacturers and cited in technical studies. Conversely, it is not an area of animal management that should be regarded lightly. It is perhaps more an art than a science.

This means that you should combine a basic knowledge of what constitutes a good diet with a fair measure of observation, and add to this a generous amount of common sense. Interestingly, of all of the nutrition experts that I have met that deal with many animal species, I do not know one that has achieved great fame as either a breeder or exhibitor. Sometimes, a considerably technical knowledge of a subject can cloud other aspects of management to the extent that the high expectations one might assume are not always realized. This is especially so in a pet-animal species in which specific objectives such as meat, fat, or milk yields are not the name of the game. With pets, the need is for all-around health, longevity, and tractability, as well as a contented animal.

Pig breeders with no scientific knowledge of foods have produced healthy pigs for as long as these animals have been domesticated. Nonetheless, there is no doubt that the extensive studies performed by food companies are of great value to the present-day owner and breeder. Commercial foods offer a number of advantages to us. For one thing, they are convenient. They are also consistent in what they contain, and they are carefully balanced to provide all of the most important ingredients—from proteins to vitamins. This takes a lot of the risk out of feeding for the person who does not start off with previous experience of the species under consideration.

However, prepared foods do have limitations. For one thing, no one can be sure that they do contain every needed constituent because every aspect of nutrition is not yet understood. There is also a psychological consideration involved in nutrition. This is often ignored altogether or regarded as an unimportant factor in feeding. Emphasis is sometimes placed too heavily on content—at the expense of the animal's enjoyment of the food. Sometimes, we get too carried away with science and forget that some of the healthiest people in the world are not those who are eating cellophane-wrapped scientifically balanced foods, with all of the unneeded color and chemical additives in them! The same is true of livestock. The prudent way to provide a nutritious diet for your pet pig is to combine the best of what science has to offer with that which is known to be natural for these animals.

THE OMNIVOROUS PIG

Your potbellied pig is an omnivore, which means its digestive system has evolved over a few hundred thousand years to be able to break down and utilize foods that are of both animal and plant origin. This is in contrast with a carnivore (a meat eater), which has difficulty digesting vegetable matter, or a herbivore (a plant eater), which cannot cope well at all with foods that are of animal origin. The digestive tracts of each of these feeding groups differ not only in

A varied diet will help to keep your porcine healthy and happy. Along with commercial brand foods, added pleasures are fresh fruits, vegetables, and dried grasses or hay.

length but also in the various bacteria they contain.

The fact that omnivores are able to digest foods of both plant and animal origin means that they are easy to feed. There are few foods that they will not accept. While this is a definite plus for you, it is not without its drawbacks in the case of any member of the family Suidae—the pigs. Contrary to their image, pigs do have a controlling mechanism that tells them when they have had enough. However, true to their image, this mechanism does not seem to work too well under captive conditions! This means that you must apply limits to what they eat rather than rely on their indicating when they have had enough. Obesity is a major problem in potbellied and other miniature pigs, so both the quantity and the quality of the food must be carefully regulated by the owner.

Pigs are extremely cosmopolitan in their feeding habits so it is not really necessary to list the foods they like, which are just about everything. They are, however, as individual in their preferences as are you or I. Some foods will be eaten with relish by all pigs; others are preferred for reasons of familiarity or taste. For example, one pig may enjoy a particular food item because it has received it from its earliest age; another pig may show little interest in the same food because it is unfamiliar with it. Likewise, all foods have a taste that is governed by their sweet content or by the amount of fats they contain. The term "sweet" should not be regarded as that contained in items such as candies but rather the natural sweeteners found in nature—the various forms of natural sugars such as glucose and its like.

Pigs really do enjoy their food, and this means you should try to supply them with a very balanced diet that is

Pigs love to eat. This pig is happy to share his treat with a friend.

When feeding your pig, make sure that it is getting quality food. Anything less will be lacking in nutritional value.

not only nutritionally adequate but also appealing to them as well. (The term "balanced" is, of course, dependent on the constituents of the food.)

THE EFFECT OF FOODS ON BODY METABOLISM

The major components of food are proteins, fats, and carbohydrates. Within foods containing them will also be found vitamins, minerals, and water. Each food item will contain these components in various quantities and ratios of one to another. Each of these constituents performs a role in the body. In all instances, an excess or deficiency of one constituent will adversely affect the performance of another. This will upset the metabolism of the pig, and this will show itself in one or more of many ways. The pig will suffer from certain illnesses or will have a reduced ability to fight any illness. It will certainly make the pig less able to reproduce healthy offspring, and in the case of the sow will severely restrict her ability to provide milk for her babies. The bone structure of a pig is clearly very dependent on sound nutrition being established from an early age. If the food is not adequate (meaning not enough in the required ratios, or an excess), this will affect growth.

A lack of enough food will not result in a smaller pig, simply a very unhealthy one. An excess of food will not create a larger pig, just a fatter one. The size to which a pig grows is only indirectly influenced by food. It is determined by genes, which give the pig an optimum potential. Whether or not this potential is reached, or what part of it is, will be determined by environmental conditions, which include the quantity and quality of the food eaten.

QUANTITY VERSUS QUALITY

The quantity and quality of a diet are interrelated. A food that has a high level of digestibility will be required in lesser amounts than one that is of low digestible content. However, a concentrated food with high digestibility is eaten quickly. The result is that while the intake may well have been ample for sound metabolism, porky still feels hungry. This is where the psychological aspect comes in. Feeding is an important part of animal socialization, very much so in gregarious species such as the pig, the dog, or the horse. If a diet does not fulfill the psychological needs of a species, it will increase the likelihood that the animal's disposition will be subject to moods brought about by psychological stress. This will make training and general care that much more difficult. The compound effects of stress brought about by both confined living and regulated diet concentrates no doubt accounts for the fact that in spite of the theoretical ideals provided to laboratory animals, their life expectancy is often only 50% that of the average for a given species.

Not only is proper nutrition important to the well being of your pig, proper shelter and cleanliness of its living quarters also play a major role in keeping it well conditioned.

When all of the various factors involved in nutrition are brought together, it can be seen that it is an extremely complex subject. It is no surprise to find that success is achieved by manipulating all factors, not simply studying the specific metabolic role that a given constituent plays—as important as this may be. This means that a pig owner feeding a theoretically inferior diet compared to that supplied by another pig owner may actually be able to produce a fitter and superior pig. This may be so if all of the other factors, such as the living quarters, exercise, general care, training, and a common-sense attitude to feeding are all of a higher standard. So what should the quantity versus quality feeding philosophy be?

Clearly, it is advantageous to supply a commercial food that has been prepared to take account of digestibility and the essential constituents needed by the pig. This will meet the metabolic needs for sound health. To this must be added a quantity of food that satisfies the pig's natural desire to forage on food for longer periods than it takes to down a bowl of concentrated food—which we have established is a very short time in the case of a pig.

But the extra food should not be heavy, starchy, or of the kind that will result in an excess of constituents such as proteins and fats. Nor should it be wholly a grain food: this will result in excess carbohydrates that will ultimately result in extra layers of fat—if this

It is difficult to state how much or how little a potbelly should be fed. It will be different for each pig, depending on factors such as age, condition, and amount of exercise.

food is not oxidized to produce only needed energy.

THE ROLE OF FOOD CONSTITUENTS

It is probable in this day and age that you are well acquainted with the role of the major food constituents. Nonetheless, for completeness, we can quickly review them.

Proteins: Proteins act as the building blocks of the body. They are oxidized during body metabolism and are broken down into units called amino acids. These acids are then put back together to form the various tissues needed by the pig—muscle, fat, blood, nervous tissue, genes, and so on. While most amino acids can be obtained from the breakdown of plant proteins, some cannot and must be supplied via animal-origin foods. Examples of protein-rich foods are meat, poultry, fish, most dairy products, seeds such as soybean, sunflower, hemp, and rape, and most nuts.

Fats: Fats are invariably found in association with proteins, so a food rich in proteins will normally also be rich in fats.

Some examples of fat-rich foods include butter, lard, and, of course, all fish oils. They provide insulation to the body, protection against buffering, and they transport other foods around the body via the blood. They are made of fatty acids, and they give food its characteristic taste. Fats are also a prime source of energy, so if a pig should find itself short of food, the first result will be that fatty tissue will be broken down to provide energy. Once the fat is depleted, the body will start breaking down the protein from the muscles; and so the pig will get thinner.

Carbohydrates: Carbohydrates are sugars in various degrees of complexity.

They are essentially the cheapest form of energy available to any animal. However, they are also important in providing bulk to the diet as well as being involved in many chemical reactions within the body cells. They are found in many foods, but the prime sources are grain and seeds.

Vitamins: We are all aware of the importance of vitamins in our diets. They are not foods as such but are vital to many reactions in the body.

As with dogs, it is important that pigs are always provided with a fresh supply of water.

They are needed to provide resistance to disease, good health, and healthy reproduction. Some can be synthesized in the gut of the pig, but most must come via food. One vitamin that is especially important to pigs is vitamin E. Vitamins of the B complex are also needed in greater quantities than is normally considered satisfactory in some mammals. However, most vitamins are important to your porcine friend. For example, if vitamin D is lacking, this adversely affects the absorption of both calcium and magnesium. Some vitamins can be stored in the body (usually in the liver), but others cannot.

Commercial foods are usually fortified with vitamins, but many do not store well and are badly affected by light, temperature, and humidity. Fresh vegetables and fruits are the most readily available natural source of these compounds, but all plant matter contains some of the vitamins. You can also purchase concentrated vitamin powders and pills, but to do so indiscriminately is to court disaster. A given problem may have nothing at all to do with vitamin deficiency, in which case the addition of supplements may only compound matters. Vitamins should be added to the diet only under veterinary advice.

Minerals: Minerals are the various elements, such as iron, calcium, copper, sulfur, potassium, magnesium, phosphorous, and many others. They are utilized in all metabolic processes. They give rigidity to cell walls and, of course, skeletal tissue. Generally, it is unlikely that your pig would ever suffer from a lack of minerals because they are so readily available in all foods. However, some of them, such as calcium, selenium, and zinc, are especially important to potbellied pigs. As a result, they are included in greater quantity in commercial foods for potbellies.

Water: All animals are dependent on staying in what is called water balance if good health is to be maintained. Whereas cats and other animals that were evolved in dry climates can regulate (thus conserve) their output (urine, sweat, milk, etc.) based on their input, a different system is used by, for example, pigs and dogs. These last two animals were evolved in areas where water was plentiful. In these animals, copious amounts of water are drunk, and, in turn, large amounts are released in the form of urine.

It is, therefore, most important that pigs always have access to fresh water; otherwise, they will quickly begin to shows signs of dehydration. This situation will be more obvious if their basic diet is largely of a commercial feed, thus of dry content.

HOW MUCH TO FEED?

In considering the amount of food your pet will need, we should first refer again to the matter of a food's digestibility.

All foods are essentially units of energy, but the usable energy contained in a given food differs one from the other. Without going into the complex aspects of gross, digestible, and metabolizable energy, the essence is that a given protein or other food may be assimilated into the body more readily than another. You cannot, therefore, use food weight as a basis for a diet across a whole range of foods. To do this would necessitate your knowing what the various energy values are for each of the foods supplied and how much energy your particular pig needs per day in relation to its body weight. Knowing the ratio of food weight to body weight for a pig's diet is thus only of use if you are restricting the diet to foods of known values, including their average moisture content. Such would be the case with commercial feeds. However, even with them, other factors will have a considerable effect on what your pet actually needs.

Pigs are not picky eaters. This little fellow and a companion have stumbled upon some bread pieces.

A pig will need more food in cold climates than it will in hot ones. A pet that receives plenty of exercise will require larger rations than one that virtually sits around the house all day.

A pig recovering from illness will need a larger-than-normal ration because it must replace the tissue used as an energy source while it was ill. There is also a genetic factor involved in that each pig is very much an individual. The efficiency of its digestive system will vary somewhat to that of another pig.

In other words, like humans, one pig will do well on a quantity of food that might be inadequate for another pig that is of similar size. The food intake of breeding sows will vary during the course of the breeding and nursing period. Given the foregoing, the following section on diet should be regarded as a *general* guideline only. You can easily tell if your pig is receiving the right amount and quality of food by simple observation. If you can just feel its ribs below a good layer of skin, this is as it should be. If you can see its bodily bone structure, it is undernourished. If it has loose folds of skin on its body, or just in front of the tail root, or on its head, neck, or jowls, it is overweight. If its belly touches the floor, it is also probably overweight.

RECOMMENDED DIET

There are now a number of special miniature-pig feeds from which you can choose. Probably the most well used is that produced by Purina Foods. This company has developed a line of foods under the brand name of Mazuri. There are three diets available: Mazuri Porcine Starter 5687, Grower 5688, and Breeder 5689. The Starter diet is for very young pigs under the age of about two months old. It is replaced by the Grower, which can be fed continually thereafter or until porky reaches breeding age, at which time the Breeder diet is recommended. You can also use a mixture of Grower and

All commercial food should be properly stored in air tight containers, and fresh food out of reach until feeding time. This pig happened by an open box of apples and got caught with his mouth full.

A special treat for a special piglet. Sweets should only be offered on a limited basis. Too much will result in an overweight pig.

Breeder as a basic diet for an adult potbelly. You would normally expect to feed these diets at the rate of about 3% of body weight. A 25-lb. youngster would require 0.75 lb. per day, while an 80-lb. adult would need 2.4 lbs.

Each of these formulated foods contains extra vitamin E, vitamins of the B complex, calcium, phosphorous, and other minerals, including selenium. They contain good roughage content and also soybean oil to enhance skin condition. Do remember that they are not typical swine foods but are specially developed for miniature pigs. Regular swine food is not suitably balanced for these pigs because its object is to put weight on pigs rapidly so they can be converted into bacon at an early age.

Heartland Exotics is another company that produces a line of foods formulated for potbellies, as well as numerous supplementary foods. Do bear in mind, however, that if you already feed one of the formulated diets, then supplements such as vitamin E and selenium may tip the balance into a negative situation. Always read the contents list on the bag of your chosen food so that you know what it contains.

Very little other foods would be required if you fed the commercial diets strictly in proportion to the pig's body weight. If you add other foods, you must reduce the formulated diet somewhat to make allowance for the nutrients in the other foods. Of course, you must also use the overall condition of your pet as the determining factor.

Other foods, which will not put too much extra weight on porky, would be fruits and vegetables such as apples, melons, and carrots. All of them contain little protein and fat and are high in water content. They can be fed on an item-by-item basis and changed each day for variety, or they can be offered as a mixed salad. Dry foods such as hay are an excellent source of roughage and will provide porky with good "psychological grazing"—as will grass.

Banana skins are a well-liked treat, the same being so of grapes, but treats can include most fruits and vegetables. Do not feed candies or other junk foods to your pet even though it would no doubt gobble them up with great relish.

With regard to the quantity of these extra foods, common sense must be the controlling factor. Supply bits of apple, plus some hay, or a few carrots and hay or grass, and see how porky looks as the weeks go by. General forage, such as hay, can be given more or less ad lib.

You could prepare a moist mash for your pet, and virtually anything could be included in it. The singular problem with this is not that it would not be nutritional if it contained animal and plant matter but that you would have no way of knowing if it contained the needed nutrients in the correct amounts and ratios. Mash feeding does require of the owner that he is much more aware of the values of the foods in the mash. However, an occasional serving of mash—as a treat—will not harm your pet.

A very large problem among potbellied pigs is obesity. Owners must check their pig's diet from time to time and adjust it according to their condition.

WHEN TO FEED

Unlike carnivores, which can consume large amounts of food at a single sitting without ill effects, herbivores and omnivores prefer to eat a little and often. This allows time for the plant-matter part of the diet to be digested slowly as it passes through the system. With this in mind, it is best to divide the total daily ration into three or four feeds. This is certainly essential for a young potbelly. Once mature, your pet will manage on two feedings a day if this is the only convenient way you can arrange things. Try to feed the meals at the same time each day because pigs, like humans, are creatures of habit. Their internal clock will tell them when it is about dinnertime, which will be eagerly awaited.

OBESITY

The obvious cause of obesity in potbellied pigs is that pet owners overfeed their little porkers, usually with too many treats of the wrong kind. While it is easy to say "do not do this," the reality is not quite that simple. Obesity tends to creep up on your pet much as it does with yourself. It will adversely affect the longevity of porky and make him much more prone to a whole range of problems, from weak limbs to internal disorders.

Once you are convinced that porky is just too fat, there is the question of how to get rid of this excess flab. What you must not do is to suddenly place your pet on a starvation diet. This can have very negative effects on both health and disposition.

Instead, look at the diet and see what items can be regarded as fattening and could thus be reduced or removed. Hamburgers, pizzas, and similar leftovers from the fast-food chains, along with candies and other junk foods, may well be part of the problem. There is nearly always one, or more, really softhearted person in the family! Next, look for any grains, seeds, or their byproducts that might have been added to the diet.

This means wheat, corn, breakfast cereals, dog chow, cookies, bread, and similar items. Depending on the quantity being given, they can either be removed from the diet or cut down drastically.

If they are not the source of the problem, then maybe you are feeding too many fruits and vegetables, so reduce them. Even forage such as hay could be a problem in association with any of the named causes, so it might be reduced also. Finally, it may just be that you are feeding too much maintenance-diet foods, and your pet is under exercised. Before I cut the fruit and veggie part of the diet, I would reduce the basic formulated ration somewhat so that a nice balance between prepared and natural foods remains intact. Do not expect the weight to drop in a few days. It may take weeks or even a few months if it is done carefully.

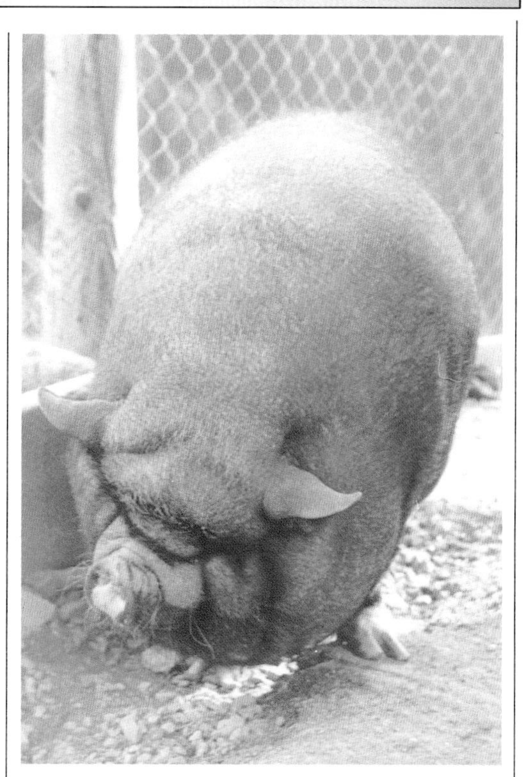

An overweight pig will find it hard to carry around its own weight and will result in a weakening of the limbs.

Obesity will put a strain on the pig's overall body and mav result in a reduced lifespan.

FOOD STORAGE

Commercial potbelly feeds are normally sold in bags that range from 10 to 50 lbs. This means that the larger size would probably last one pet for about two and one-half months, give or take a little depending on the animal's size and other factors discussed (activity level, etc.). It is, therefore, very important that the food is stored in a cool, dry cupboard in order to preserve its nutritional value. Mold will grow on damp food, while food that is exposed to sunlight will quickly lose the vitamin value it contains. Food must always be safeguarded against the risk of being fouled by vermin. If this is ever suspected, it is best to throw out the remaining food in the bag.

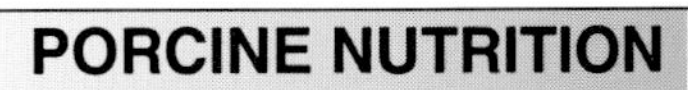

Good nutrition will help your pig stay healthy and content.

Grains are an important source of carbohydrates, which is an energy food source.

All other food should be fresh and washed before being fed to porky. Forget forever all the stories that pigs will eat any old food regardless of its state; they will do this only when forced to by near starvation, and they would likely become ill as a result. Always remember that potbellied pigs are not your regular farm livestock, but miniature versions.

Like all other "scaled-down" animals, they may appear to eat like their larger cousins, but they do have very sensitive stomachs that are easily upset. Feed only quality foods, and this will be one less problem to worry about.

Finally, when selecting a feed supplier, be sure to be discriminating. The one favored with your business should be doing a healthy trade in livestock foods. He should not have sacks of food, some of which have burst their contents onto the floor and been left there to encourage vermin, all over the place. There should be no open sacks of food—any food sold by loose weight should be in proper containers. The dealer should want you to have the correct food. If it is not stocked, he should order it for you, maybe against prepayment initially. If he tries to sell you standard farmyard-pig feed and states that "it's just as good," take your business elsewhere.

Never go looking for the cheapest feed. If the quality is good and the service likewise, then don't quibble about the price—it will be fair if the dealer has been chosen wisely.

The Psychology of Training

If I were asked what is the singular most important subject for any novice pet owner to understand, I would say the psychology of training a pet. This would be qualified by adding "if it was any of those pets that could suffer as a result of not being trained." From a pure popularity-standpoint, the pets in question are the dog, large parrots, and the house pig. I would put the subject of the psychology of training ahead of any other aspect of husbandry for these pets. Yes, even ahead of nutrition. Now I will explain why: these particular pets are potentially dangerous as well as being destructive to furniture if they are not trained. If the pet is destructive, what often happens is that ultimately the pet is banished to an outside enclosure, passed on to an animal shelter, or by other means disposed of. If the pet is banished to a kennel or outside enclosure because it is a "failed" pet, you can just bet that in nine cases out of ten its nutrition will then suffer—as will most other aspects of its general care. Essentially, if you cannot enter into a very personal relationship with an animal, human nature is such that the animal will be neglected to a greater or lesser degree. In other words, all aspects of its care are highly dependent on the relationship (affection) you have with your pet, and that relationship is determined by the extent of the pet's training.

If a dog owner, parrot owner, or pet pig owner is not prepared to devote the time required for training, then they should forget owning these particular animals—they will be disasters just waiting to happen. For this reason, this subject has been divided into two chapters; thus it has the largest coverage in this book. I will not jump straight into instructive training but will try to shape the way you think about the training and then discuss practical means of using the theory learned. Your future enjoyment of your porcine pal is contingent on whether or not you can train it to live with you in the confines of your home in a mutually satisfactory manner.

AN OVERVIEW OF TRAINING

Potbellied pigs are "new" pets, and much is now being written about them. Included in this literature are many magazine articles and book chapters devoted to training. Such texts are excellent, but some of them do imply that a pig is totally different from a dog, a horse, a parrot, or any other animal, when it comes to being trained. This I would have to disagree with. Each of these animals may well have certain limitations on what they can actually be taught or in the degree of difficulty in doing so. They may have limitations that are a result of their physical conformation. They may also have an inherent predisposition to react in certain ways (instinct), but the ways in which they learn, which is what you are interested in, are exactly the same.

Intelligence and other aspects of the brain are evolutionary traits. The intelligence of all mammals has a common path, while response to

As with dogs, training is a very important aspect of a pig's life, especially if it is to become a well mannered house pet.

stimuli has evolved as a trait common to all organisms. In other words, whether we are talking about a dog, a horse, a bird, a mouse, or a potbellied pig, it learns in exactly the same manner: it reacts to the world around it exactly the same as any other animal does when you are considering basic traits. For example, it is said that a pig gets frightened when you lean over its head because this is how predators attack it. But this reaction is equally true of the predator itself. It is also true of all birds. It is said that pigs are different from dogs because pigs will run away when startled, but so will a dog—or even a wolf pack—if it is unsure of the nature and degree of the threat confronting it. In other words, we must not get too carried away by observations that might distort what is perceived to be a difference between animals. What we are seeing in herd and predator/pack situations is the consequence of both their instincts *and* what they have learned—not *how* they learned to behave in a particular manner in the first place.

It therefore seems more appropriate to consider training from a more basic standpoint rather than in relation to a particular species. Modifications must, of course, be made to take into account the physical ability of the pet in question, but this does not affect the underlying philosophy of how it can be trained. Forget that porky is a pig, and think of him as an entity that will respond to given situations in a very predictable manner (generally). Always remember that your pet is an individual, and its predisposition for learning and traits such as friendliness, aggression, and trust are inherent to it as an individual. The fact that most of a litter are bold and friendly does not mean that all of the litter will be so to the same degree.

Bear in mind also that another word for training is learning; the owner teaches and the pet learns. If you are a bad teacher, your pet will learn very little, only negative things. You must be honest enough to recognize and change, or at least suppress, your own failings—we all have them.

THE BASICS OF TRAINING

There is no shortage of different methods of training, some of which are named for the trainer who advocates them. They are usually very good because they are all based on the same theory, even if the way in which that theory is practiced differs from one method to another. You can, of course, read a book on how to train porky and follow it to the letter. This requires no understanding of why you are doing what you are doing.

Alternatively, you can learn the theory of response manipulation of traits, and then apply it to your training program. This is far superior because you can apply it to any situation with which you are confronted. You will understand why your pet reacts the way it does and why you are not really any different, just more capable of working things out.

Essentially, all training methods are based on three simple fundamentals: that any animal responds to any situation in a positive, neutral (passive), or negative manner. If you can manipulate an animal's response to coincide with your wishes, you are able to train that animal. Forget the words good and bad because to your pet they have no meaning whatsoever. To porky, everything around him is a stimulus—to a greater or lesser degree. Your pet reacts to stimuli; it doesn't rationalize reasons but simply reacts in one way or another. That

Piglets need to become accustomed to people at an early age. If not socialized, it is one more obstacle for a new pig owner to overcome before any other training processes can begin.

reaction will be instinctive in the absence of training but will be modified if training has taken place.

TRAINING THE TUTOR

The first thing you must do in preparation for training is to detach your mind from the tendency to view your pet in human terms. The fact is that it does not think like you, it does not moralize as you do, it cannot understand your language, and it cannot learn other than by what happens to it at any given moment. It can relate to the past, and this will determine its reactions to any given situation in the present. If there is no past precedent to modify its reactions, it will fall back on instinct to determine how it should act. You must view all aspects of training your pig in a simple framework of response to different stimuli, not in terms of applying rational thought to the response—as you might do. You can chastise a child for something it did hours before, and it will relate your annoyance to that past incidence and will understand. You can promise your child a goody if it does a set chore in the future, and it will understand. Your pet cannot relate in this manner, which is a fact that must always shape the way you react. Porky cannot move up to your level of intelligence, but you can move down to his. This is the crux of your being a good or bad tutor. In the vast majority of instances, if your pet becomes a really obnoxious animal, the total blame for this goes to you and nobody else. Never look for excuses because the problem is you, not your porcine pal. Do not try to kid yourself otherwise as so many owners do.

Remember also that there is no place in training for sentiment. It is the root cause of many problem pets. This is not to suggest that heavy-handed methods are required: they are invariably counterproductive. What it means is that having determined a course of action with your pet, you must persist in it; otherwise you will inadvertently only make the situation worse. Never blame your pet for actions that you have instilled in it because you could not resist the temptation to give in to sentimentality. Deep affection and trust are the cornerstones of good training, but do not confuse love of your pet with sentimentality as applied to training.

Positive reinforcement is important when training porky. If training is handled in a negative manner, it will result in an unhappy, poorly trained pet.

HOW DOES PORKY LEARN?

A major difference that separates mammals and birds from reptiles, amphibians, and fishes, in terms of intelligence, is the power of memory. The better your memory the more you can learn. Your porcine friend learns by applying that which it has experienced to that which was inherited (instinct). The one modifies or overrides the other. When your pet is confronted with a given situation, it will scan its memory for a suggestion of how it should react. If there is no previous experience to relate to, it will respond by instinct; and the instincts of all animals are the same at a very basic level. For example, if they are under threat, they will either take flight or they will turn around and face the threat.

The nature of the threat, the situation, and the age of the threatened animal will determine which course of action is taken. A young pig under attack will run (instinct), but with maturity and experience (memory) of different foes it may decide to turn and become the aggressor itself—attack being a good form of defense. Another word for experience is learning, so we come back to the matter of memory recall.

As your piglet grows, its life is a whole series of happenings, and what does happen will determine what is

This piglet is enjoying a rest under a warm stove. Early training will help to ensure that it does not become unruly and destructive.

placed into the memory. If the action (stimulus) is consistent, the pet will react in a consistent manner. If the action is variable, the pet may react likewise because it is not sure which of its actions will be most appropriate for its general well being. It becomes confused just as you would, and a confused animal, be it a pig or yourself, may not react in a way that is deemed correct or which proves to be to its best advantage.

The greater the number of new situations a pet is placed in, the larger the number of memories it has available for recall. Reaction to a stimulus is thus also influenced by environment. For example, in your locality your piglet may walk really confidently by your side on his leash. However, taken to downtown Manhattan or a similar metropolis, things could change dramatically if it has never been exposed to heavy traffic, lots of people, and noises in close proximity to it.

In such a situation, the emotion of fear (an instinct), may override the training, so what is in the memory is ignored. In training your little piglet, you must therefore always bear in mind that while that which is learned can override instinct, instinct can also suppress that which is learned. It all depends on the environment (meaning any situation that the piglet has never experienced before) and the extent of exposure to it. A piglet that reacts favorably with you and other family members may become nervous or aggressive when strangers come into your home. Again, this is a new situation for porky. When scanning its memory, it cannot find the answer to how it should react, so it may do so in an uncharacteristic manner.

SOME TRAINING TERMS

It is useful if you understand the meaning of certain terms that are

Once trained to walk on a leash, piggy can accompany you almost anywhere – even to the beach on mild days.

used in animal psychology. In understanding them, you can work out for yourself various ways of applying them, though examples will be given.

Threshold: This is the level of stimulus that must be received in order to elicit a response. The stimulus may be minimal or severe, depending on the imprinting intensity of the behavior that is required to be changed. For example, a pig has a low threshold for eating, which means it takes little stimulus in order to get it to eat. However, this example is a variable threshold because once the pig is satiated, the threshold rises. For this reason, the use of treats is not always the best training aid because the animal's response will depend on how satiated it is at the time of a training session. Nonetheless, treats are generally reliable for pigs who always seem hungry! Most instincts have a low threshold (dogs to chase, cats to stalk, herd animals to run, and so on). This means that they can sometimes be difficult to counteract by training. Thus it is a case of controlling or manipulating them via training (learning).

Reinforcer: This is any stimulus that will tend to reinforce a given action. There are three basic forms of reinforcer: one is primary, the second is discriminative, and the third is internalized. A primary enforcer would be to spank your pet (punishment) or to give it a big hug (affection). A discriminative reinforcer would be the use of words such as 'no' or 'good boy.' In these instances, the primary enforcer is not needed because it is implied by the tone of your voice—so it may still elicit the same response. An internalized reinforcer is the condition whereby

By exposing a pig to many different environments when young, it will be better able to handle different surroundings and situations when it gets older.

the action itself reinforces the pattern of behavior. In other words, it becomes a habit (which can be desirable or undesirable—depending on your viewpoint).

Generalization: This term is used for a pattern of behavior that widens without having received specific stimuli to do so. It is a very important aspect of animal behavior. There are many examples that could be used, but a few will suffice. One is the word 'no.' When it is first used with porky, the response will be to a very specific undesirable action. However, the same word can later be used for any undesirable action, and it will have the same effect. It will have generalized from a specific action to any comparable action. This might be termed simple generalization, so let us look at a complex example.

Your pet is taken to a friend's home, and while it is there it by chance happens to be badly frightened by a dog that leaps at it from its dog bed. Sometime later you purchase a new bed for your little friend and are at a loss to understand why he refuses to use it. Indeed, it seems to elicit a fear response in porky. What has happened is that the fright from the dog became associated with the dog bed as well. With time, the fear begins to generalize to any other item that may only remotely resemble the original dog bed. In severe cases, this generalization may spread to almost any item, or even a room, or place, because one thing may be associated with another from the original room or place.

A piglet has a good memory. Only reinforce habits which are satisfactory and discourage those that are not.

Negative generalizations can thus be extremely frustrating to overcome because you are not always sure what the original problem was, or even that there was one, or when it happened. There is, of course, a good side to generalization because it can work the other way. If your pet is really happy in a given situation, it can generalize on things and places that it associates with that happy feeling. Other examples of this behavior pattern are in respect to sitting on a chair, which generalizes to sitting on the sofa, and then the bed. Likewise, if a piglet is allowed to pull and tear at a piece of old cloth, this action will generalize to any piece of cloth, which could be your best clothes, the curtains, or cushions. In other words, generalization can create habits, both good and bad. Only sound training will restrict the extent of bad habits.

Counterconditioning: This is any stimulus that tends to weaken or stop a given action by replacing it with a desirable alternative. For example, there are three ways you can change a given action. They are

Piglets and friend enjoying an afternoon nap. If piggies are permitted to sleep on certain furnishings when young and will not be allowed to when fully grown, it will be best not to let them do so from the onset.

by punishment, by removal of causal stimuli, or by counterconditioning. Let us say that your pig has developed the habit of nudging you when you sit down. It has reached the point where the pig is becoming a real pest at doing this. We will consider the ways you can deal with the matter and then why it happened in the first place.

You could simply whack porky on the nose every time he nudges you. There is no denying the fact that this will bring about a very rapid positive response (from your viewpoint). Discipline is the fastest way to bring about a behavioral change. As a result, it is most often used by those who do not understand the psychology of training. It is also the last resort of a good trainer (violence being the last resort of a tired mind!). Its problem is that while it might elicit the desired response to a particular action, it is totally unpredictable in how it will generalize.

Your pet may stop nudging you, but it may also become fearful of approaching you at all, which is not what you had intended. Furthermore, while porky may respect your punishment, it does not follow that the reaction will be the same with other people. If you tell them to swat his nose your pet may well stop—but then again it may react in an aggressive manner and bite them or try to "charge" them. As I said, discipline is unpredictable so it is not a wise tool for a trainer.

The second way to stop the unwanted behavior is by removal of the reinforcer—in this case, you! This approach is hardly appropriate to the situation just discussed but works when porky is forever raiding the garbage can.

The third and best way to overcome the problem is to countercondition. But, unfortunately, this approach is also the most difficult. The theory of the method is that your pet cannot behave in two different ways at the same time. It cannot be reaching to nudge you if it is sitting still doing nothing.

If you ignore the nudges every single time without fail but fuss over your pet when it is sitting still in front of you, your pig is intelligent enough to slowly get the message that being fussed over only results when it is not nudging you. Your counterconditioning will reinforce the desired action while making the undesired action a waste of your pig's time. There will be no reinforcer to the habit of nudging. Additionally, you might move your leg out of the way or say "no" at the moment the nudge takes place. This is a discipline, but it is much lower on the scale than a whack because no physical discomfort is felt by the pig.

But it would be altogether better that this habit had never developed in the first place so we must consider how it was developed. At some point, porky nudged you—an exploratory action. Your response was to fuss over him and maybe even give a treat—thus reinforcing the action. It seemed really good at first because it was a means of bonding between the both of you. The problem is that you let it go beyond that and become a bad habit. Every time your pet wants your attention it nudges you and you fuss over it or give it a treat. Having realized that this is the way to command attention, porky will now try the ploy on every other person. Depending on the individual's actions, porky will be a pest or he will leave the person alone if the desired response is not forthcoming. This is why some pets are a pest to one family member but not to another (when an action gets no result). Your pig is astute enough to know that failure with one person does not mean failure with another. Only when all responses are fruitless will the habit be dropped altogether.

Schedule Stretching: Now, here's the difficult part of counterconditioning. It is called schedule stretching. If an action, whether it be desirable or

'Consistency' is the key word when training young piglets. If your responses to their actions differ from one day to the next, the result will be very confused pupils.

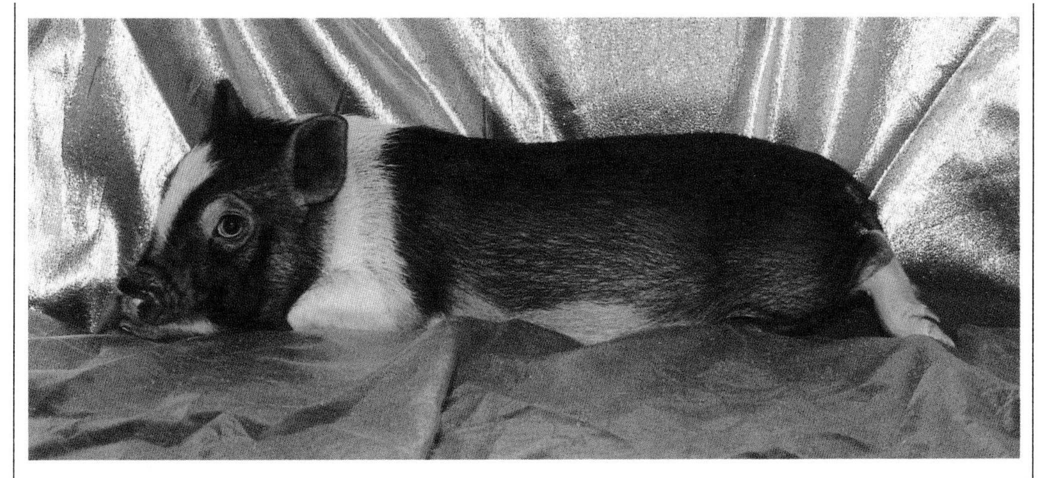

A pig that knows exactly what is expected of it will result in a happy, content, and obedient companion.

undesirable, is to become part of your pet's behavioral repertoire, it will initially require regular reinforcing. However, with the passage of time the number of reinforcers needed declines quite dramatically. Ultimately, only occasional "topping up" is needed to maintain the action. This means that, taking the case of nudging, you only need to be lax in your actions on a few occasions in order to maintain the behavior pattern. The alternate pattern you have introduced will, of course, be part of the repertoire, so you will end up with two behavior patterns. The pig will use both.

Again, as in generalizing, the pattern works both ways. If your pet is taught (bribed!) to respond to a treat, you will find that the action will still be featured even when no treat is given. Praise will be sufficient reward, but a treat now and then will reinforce the behavior. Here you see schedule stretching being combined with internalized reinforcement to become a habit. The more pleasurable the action, the lesser the need for a reinforcer.

Learned Helplessness: This is the last term we will discuss, and it is another very important subject in the training of your pet. A fundamental essential for any animal is that it must be able to determine events based on its own actions. The less it is able to do this the less it can respond to stimuli in any predictable manner. If a pig is disciplined for an action on one occasion but not on another, or, worse still, is praised for that same action, it will become totally confused. The net result is that it cannot make a decision because it has lost control over the consequences of its own actions.

When severe instances of this are seen, the results are extremely variable and very sad. One pet may simply become very aggressive and attempt to attack its owner or the person who is trying to apply the discipline. Another pet may run and hide in a corner, in total fear. Another may simply lay down, tremble, and urinate. These situations are very common occurrences in dogs, and, sadly, they will be seen in many pigs as pigs gain in popularity. You might not be able to conceive of how anyone could be so ignorant of what they are doing, but ponder the following.

An owner comes home from work and normally fusses over his pet when it runs to greet him. Another day, the owner is in a really bad mood and responds to the piggy by shouting and whacking it. The pig approaches the owner again in a more submissive manner but is promptly given an even harder smack. The next day, things are better, and the pig is fussed over. This totally inconsistent behavior eventually results in the piggy urinating in the home when it is being disciplined. This prompts an even more negative response from the owner, who ejects the pet into the yard or, worse, rubs the pet's nose in the urine. Now the pet has no idea of why it is being disciplined—is it for greeting the owner, is it for being submissive, or is it because it has urinated? A total breakdown in its behavior patterns is now well underway. In some bad homes, this type of situation may be inflicted on the pet by more than one family member. For example, the husband allows the piggy to go on the chair, but the wife smacks it for doing so because she does not want it on the furniture. They argue and shout, and this merely makes the pet even more frightened, insecure, and confused.

Many pigs love to go for a ride. Car training at an early age will make piggy a calm, stress free passenger.

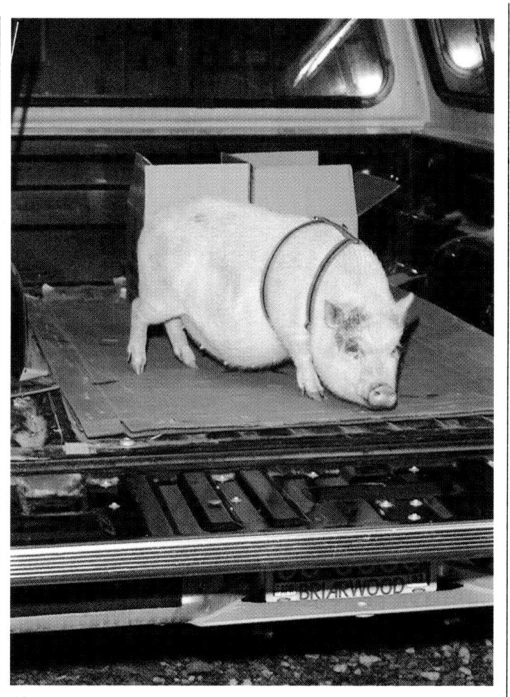

If being taken out in the back of a pick-up, to prevent any injuries to the pig, it should be confined to a crate that will be unable to slide around in the back of a truck.

It will not come to them when they call it, so this results in another whack for lack of obedience—which merely reinforces the pig's reluctance to approach them the next time they call it. I am sure you are familiar with this type of pattern because you can see it in families where children are abused in just the same manner, and they react just as any other animal will. However, while this is an example of extreme learned helplessness resulting from improper and inconsistent use of discipline, do not overlook the fact that similar reactions can be created by excessively fussing over a pet.

A pet that is forced to be held and cuddled when it does not want to be is in a situation where it cannot determine events. If it struggles to get free, the owner may smack it to make it submissive—so that it can be fussed over. There is no malice intended, quite the opposite, but the owner's actions will result in a very negative stimulus being given to the pig for the act of being picked up. Some pets just do not like to be fussed over excessively; others will take it non-stop. It all comes back to the matter of individuality. For one particular pet, a given stimulus—being picked up and fussed over—is a negative, yet in another pet it results in a very positive reaction.

UTILIZING PSYCHOLOGY

From the foregoing, you will appreciate that it is not necessary for you to "think pig" —or dog or horse—when you are training these animals. Yes, it helps to know a little about their natural lifestyles as this gives you an insight into instincts and how they form part of these animals' survival strategies: not how they think but how they react to stimuli. We have established that they cannot begin to understand how we think, and it is presumptuous of us to assume that we know how they think. At best, we can learn how they react and use this knowledge to our, and, hopefully, their advantage when living in close confinement within our society.

In utilizing psychology, you must think before any course of action is taken. You must especially remove your emotional feelings when reacting to a an undesirable situation, but you can let emotion flow when reinforcing success. This is actually very important because your piglet learns more from achieving success in a behavior than from failure. When you run up against a problem, try to work it out in terms of positive or negative stimuli. This is by no means easy. Breaking long-established habits is far harder than avoiding them in the first place or correcting them before they become too deeply embedded in a behavior pattern.

Praise, when a pig acts favorably, will award you better results than only punishing the pig when it has done wrong.

Practical Training

In this chapter we can consider a number of behaviors, desirable and undesirable, and use knowledge gained from the previous chapter to achieve your training objectives. I have concentrated on behaviors that are most commonly desired or that are problems in day-to-day living with a porcine pet. Let us first consider some general advice.

1. Training should start as soon as your piglet is taken home. Do not allow time for undesirable behaviors to start.

2. When training your pet, do it when there is a minimum of other distractions that might bring his instincts to the fore. For example, porky is far less likely to begin bonding with you if lots of other people are around and there are other noises that will elicit a fear instinct.

3. Never let any training lesson become too long. Piggie's powers of concentration will wane, and this will result in boredom and frustration.

4. Always end formal training sessions in a positive way, never on a down note. If piggy has flunked its first lesson, that's OK—give it lots of praise. At least its memory of the lesson will be positive.

5. Never apply a fixed timeframe regarding how fast an objective is to be reached. Failure in this matter will tend to frustrate you and maybe tempt you into pressing on too quickly, which might frustrate your pet.

6. Always begin training sessions with a task that your pig can perform with ease. Give lots of praise: this sets up the mood for the task ahead.

7. If things are not going well and you can sense your own annoyance or frustration, stop the lesson. Give praise and call it a day, ending with a simple task if possible.

8. If you have young children in your home, they will need training as well if they are not to undo, or at least make more difficult, that which you are trying to achieve.

9. Your piglet will never understand the words that you use, but it can understand tone. The simpler the instruction the easier it will be for porky to associate the tone and volume with the desired reaction. Do not bore and frustrate it with a load of wordy, lengthy instructions. Bear in mind that your pet has good hearing, so you do not need to scream your head off as many people seem to do in dog training classes! Do talk softly and often when not training your little friend: this will soothe him.

10. When things are going badly, always remind yourself that you are the problem—not your pet. Porky does not know what you want done so it is up to you to think up a better way of communicating what you require.

COMING TO YOU

The very first behavior that you should achieve is that of having your pet come to you. This may not be a problem if the breeder has done his work in socializing piggy; but, even so, a piglet, like any other juvenile, may be insecure when moving away from home. Give your pet a name that is short and easy to pronounce. Use it constantly. Patience is to be the greatest attribute of a trainer. Do not force your attentions on piggy. Let him come to you whenever possible, and always lavish praise for

Piglets' training and socialization should begin as soon as possible. Well-trained and loved pigs will make wonderful and enjoyable companions for people of all ages.

Until porky is litterbox trained, it is best to keep it confined in an area that is easy to clean when accidents occur.

this behavior. You may indeed coax your pet with a tidbit.

Kneel down so that you do not appear intimidating. Never grab at a piglet, and always move in a slow and deliberate manner so that porky can see what you are doing. This applies to your hands especially. If the pet is rather nervous, it is better to restrict its potential means of flight. I find that the bathroom is a good place to work with newly acquired animals as there are few places for them to run and hide behind or under. The pets are also quite close to me relative to the situation in other rooms. Never let your pet's coming to you be a negative stimulus. For example, even when porky has grown up, this must always be a source of great pleasure to him. What sometimes happens with owners is that they call their pets to them in order to tell them off for gobbling up a bag of apples or for some other undesirable action that happened ten or so minutes earlier. What then transpires is that the pet associates the discipline with going to the owner, not with eating the apples. Remember the comment about pets learning from the present moment, not from the past. What you do in the present is what they will recall from their memory the next time you call them to you. Coming willingly to you is the most important of all behavior patterns that your pig can develop—as simple as it might seem.

It means that a bond is being formed, and until this happens worthwhile training progress can never be achieved. The closer the bond between you and porky the more your pet will want to please you—and accept discipline without any adverse side effects.

Never call porky to you in order to administer medicines because this also registers a negative in its mind. Go and pick up your pet, and then give him the medicine.

TOILET TRAINING

Toilet training will apply to both the home and yard situation. In the home, a litterbox will be used. In the yard, you may or may not wish to restrict the area in which porky attends to his needs.

You are aware that pigs live for the present moment. This means that in order to tackle any aspect of their training, you must have a high degree of control over what they do at any given moment. Otherwise, you cannot manipulate what is placed in their "memory box."

Your little piglet will use a litterbox not because he understands that it is a toilet but because you imprint in his memory that this is the place to urinate and defecate. The very act of using the box becomes an internalized habit that develops from initial reinforcement. In order for this to happen, you must understand when a piglet is most likely to want to relieve itself and how to train it to use the litterbox. The younger the piglet, the less control it has over its bowel movements.

As a guide, it will wish to relieve itself about 20 minutes after it has eaten and much sooner than this after it has just awakened from sleep. It will also wish to relieve itself after, or even during, periods of excited play. Unlike a cat or puppy, you will get no indication of its desire to use a toilet, so you must be diligent in considering the timings mentioned and the following advice. At the stated times, you should take porky to the litterbox and place him in it. Gently encourage him to stay there for at least a few seconds. Once he has used the litterbox, remove soiled material and replace with fresh shavings, but leave a small amount of fecal matter at the far end of the box (so porky can smell it but does not have to walk on it). Generally, you should place your pet in the box about five to six times a day until he is using it consistently. Always give praise when piggy uses its box—even when it is an adult.

It is altogether better that until your pet has become litterbox trained, it is restricted as to where it can wander in your home. You cannot influence its behavior if it has the freedom to use any room as a toilet. Once it is trained, you can allow it greater freedom. However, be sure to place additional boxes at strategic places around the home so that there is never any problem in your pet reaching one when the need arises. This alone will overcome many problems that may otherwise happen as a result of little "accidents." By the time a piglet is about four months old, it has much greater control over its bowels. At six months of age, it may be able to control its toilet needs for almost a day, but do not count on it. Much depends on the food it is eating, its general health, and its sex. (Unspayed gilts will not control their bowels, especially urine, as they come into heat).

TOILET TRAINING PROBLEMS

The most common problem that is experienced by all owners (including trainers), is when the pet starts to

As with dogs, house training is one of the most crucial matters to be dealt with if kept inside. This piggy is resting with two of her favorite companions.

urinate or defecate on the carpet or in places other than where it should go. Unlike cats, whose toiletry habits are part of their predatory survival strategy (they cover fecal matter to disguise their presence), this is not so with herd animals. The effect of this fact is that pigs are much more likely to forget their toilet training unless it is very deeply imprinted in their behavior pattern. For one thing, while the removal of a cat box to another spot will prompt the cat to seek it out, this is not so with most pigs. They will simply go to the place where the box used to be and attend to their needs as usual. Manipulating toilet instincts is thus more difficult in herd animals than in predators.

Once a pig has fouled a given spot in your home, the spot will leave a smell unless it is very carefully cleaned and de-scented with a suitable deodorizer. This, however, is not as easy as it may seem. The scent may linger in a carpet some distance from the actual spot and can be picked up by the pig's excellent scenting ability. Sometimes the owner may not even notice a small puddle, so porky uses this spot again—thus reinforcing the behavior. The scent may even be in the chairs or other furniture, so you will appreciate the potential magnitude of this problem.

Like dogs and cats, pigs can be house trained and will let you know when they need to go out to attend to their needs.

You do, however, have a few options to resolve the situation. The simplest, and by far the most effective, is removal of the reinforcer. In other words, do not allow the pet into the room that was soiled for some time. Clean the carpet and furniture as best you can. If the room has no door, try to seal it off from piggy. Alternatively, if there is no litterbox in that room, place one in it and retrain porky to use it. You can place food bowls where the piglet was known to have fouled, but I do not regard this as either a practical or desirable option. The theory is that your pet will not want to foul an area nearby its feed bowl, which is true. But placing food bowls all over the place is both inconvenient and not a logical behavioral solution. You must change the basic behavior pattern itself.

If you catch piggy in the act of fouling places other than in its box, this author would try to reach the pet without frightening it, then transport it to the box and praise it. Chances are it will not continue relieving itself; nonetheless, you are concentrating on what you wish to reinforce and, with patience, you will be successful. An alternative strategy is to say "no" in a stern voice, which is a practice advocated by some authorities. I dislike this method because it is totally negative. It does not place any message into the pet's memory other than that it should not relieve itself, which is obviously a very natural thing for it to do. Hearing such a negative stimulus is likely to frighten the pet, which will simply run away

A pig should be provided with a bed of its own, as well as some toys. This will help to keep it occupied and out of trouble elsewhere in the home.

from you because it will not associate the command with fouling the carpet—but with defecation. The next time, it will simply try to relieve itself where you cannot see it: under a chair, behind it, and so on. It thus does not really address your objective and is an example, in this instance, of using a stimulus on the wrong occasion.

Other factors that may contribute to weakening an established pattern are if the litterbox is allowed to become dirty or if the pet simply outgrows it in terms of size. No animal that I know of enjoys walking in its own excrement. It (e.g., a barnyard pig or caged animal) is invariably forced to do so because it has no options to do otherwise (bad management). Your pig is not as flexible as a cat or dog, so it cannot turn around in quite the same small space. If it has difficulty in turning, it will either be disinclined to use the box or will stand in the front but attend to its business outside of the box.

If your pet starts to become really difficult, or if he is difficult from the outset, you may find that crate or pen training is the easiest way to litterbox train him. With this method, the pet has very restricted space in which to move around. The pen or crate must be large enough to accommodate sleeping space and litterbox. The pig will not wish to foul its bed so it will utilize the box.

It is important that the bedding material is not of the same material as that used in the box. Use blankets or similar material for bedding; otherwise, the pet may sleep in the box and foul the bed area! Place the piglet in the crate or pen after it has eaten, and leave it there until it has relieved itself before letting it out for a run.

In order to train piggy to go outside to attend to its needs, you must take it out for short periods at the same times suggested for litterbox training. When it performs as required, it should be highly praised so that the message relayed to its memory is, in

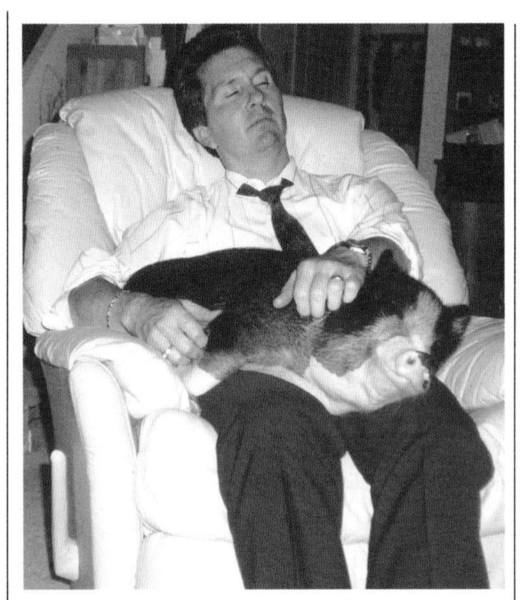

This pig is truly part of the family. Only through patience, attention, and love will you beget this type of friend.

effect, "Go outside, attend to a natural instinct, and get lots of praise—a good way to get fussed over." Try to be very consistent in all aspects of toilet training because piggy, like you, will tend to want to relieve himself at much the same times each day, assuming his feeding regimen is also at regular times. If you want your pet to use a particular spot in your yard, fence it in; and take porky there each time. Always try to stay with piggy until he has adopted the behavior pattern required.

UNDESIRABLE HABITS

The following is a discussion of the more common problems that are encountered with a house-pet piggy.

Tears Clothing and Other Materials: Pigs really enjoy foraging about. It is a very natural thing for them to do. In the wild, they will tear up strands of grass and push them into a pile to form a cozy bed. If they are not provided with a warm bed and lots of things to amuse themselves with, they will seek these kinds of things out for themselves. Provide them with newspapers, fruit branch twigs, pieces of cardboard, or dog chews. These things will help satisfy their need to root around. Of course, a rooting box is an absolute essential for a pig. If one is not available, piggy will likely feel the need to root among pillows, cushions, and other materials. Never play tug of war with your piggy using any form of old material as doing so will generalize to all material. To your pet, a good suit or dress is really no different from the old rag that you use when you play with him.

Very often this habit can be traced back to an event in the pet's past. Maybe it pulled on a curtain or dragged a sock around the room. You thought this was amusing then; but as it generalizes to other things with the passage of time, it stops becoming amusing. Always observe what your piglet is doing, and consider whether you will be as happy letting it do that when it is far larger and more powerful. When it is a baby, simply take things away from it that you feel it could generalize. No discipline is needed on a tiny piglet; but if a problem starts to emerge as it grows, you must take the article in question away from him and at the say time say "no" in a firm voice.

Sometimes, piggie will focus on your clothes, such as underwear, as they carry a strong scent of you. Here, removal of the reinforcer is the answer. Keep things away from porky so that the habit cannot be reinforced. Boredom may be another reason for the problem. Again, this comes back to ensuring that your pet has things with which it can amuse itself while you are away from the home.

Timidity or Nervousness: Timidity or nervousness may occur because the breeder or seller did not socialize the piglet before you became its owner. Either of these conditions may also be present if the pig has been bred from poor or nervous stock, in which case the trait is inherent. It may also be the case that you or other family members are not bonding well enough with porky or that you are counteracting your good work with negatives. Finally, timidity or nervousness may be due to something in the environment. Maybe another household pet, such as a dog, is frightening piggy—or did so when the pig first came into your care. You should realize that there are many reasons, both in the present and in the past, that may have created, or made worse, either of these conditions.

Very often, pet owners look for a simple solution to a problem that is very complex. Sometimes the problems can never be resolved because, in truth, the owner simply isn't suited to his pet, or any other one that requires affection and great patience in its general care. However, we will assume that this is not the case in your household.

Think carefully about what is happening in your home. Is the pet timid all the time or only on certain occasions—when a noisy child is present, when people are around, when your dog is close by? Do all of the family members love porky or does one of them dislike him? Do the children (or you) tease him? Any of these situations could be the source of the problem. If you again come up

If a large amount of time is spent with your piglets, it will result in happy, playful, and outgoing pets.

with a blank, then it is most probable that you simply do not spend enough time making friends with your little pal or are trying to rush things—and in the process frightening it.

I cannot overstress the fact that initial bonding is the cornerstone to all that follows—and you cannot rush this process. The more time you spend with your pet the sooner it will become relaxed in your presence. You do not have to be handling it all the time, but if it is physically near you, this is how bonding begins. Only when it is really relaxed with you can you begin to tackle other social problems that it may have. You must be able to touch any part of its body without this action eliciting a fear response. If you cannot, your bonding is well short of desirable. All pets enjoy being soothingly rubbed and stroked, but try to notice those areas that your piggy especially seems to like.

Coax it to you with a tidbit, and let it sniff you. Do this often and sit down with it; do not intimidate it by standing over it. Never chase it around the room in order to catch it, but wait for it to come to you. If it is very nervous when you obtain it, you must confine it to a small area. Otherwise, it will simply run and hide (but this would suggest that you purchased the pet from the wrong person).

Socialization with other household pets should be supervised at first, to assure that all get along and that there are no problems. These three fellows are getting along just fine.

Once porky is totally at ease with you is the time to see if it is equally at ease, by the same process, with other family members. This may pinpoint the problem person. If the pet is happy with all family members, then take it to other rooms in your home and see if it appears nervous. Slowly but surely, by ensuring that it always associates rooms and things with good happenings, you can overcome nervousness or timidity.

Aggressiveness with Strangers: This situation will occur either because a stranger has at some point frightened or hurt porky (with or without your knowledge) or simply through lack of familiarity with strangers. First, unless your pet is totally at ease with *you*, it is most unlikely that it will ever be relaxed with strangers.

To overcome fear of strangers, you must invite to your home people whom you know that really love animals. They should not attempt to fuss over your pet right away but sit as near as possible to it and just talk with you. They might then offer it a favorite tidbit and very slowly place their arm or hand near it so that it can sniff at them. If all goes well, they may be able to stroke porky. From that point onward, success is progressively developed.

The more often strangers meet porky the better. Once your pet is trained to walk well on a harness, it should be taken to places where

If a pig is expected to act favorably with strangers, it should be given the chance to meet many different people when young. This pig is enjoying some friendly attention.

progressively more people will be encountered. It will steadily become more confident and will resent strangers less and less, and it will allow them to stroke its body (in an area that you think is advisable). Like so many other problems with pigs, the basic cause is simply either a lack of affection or the fact that the pet has not been exposed to a given situation in such a way that it is not a frightening experience. All things must be done on a consistently built-up basis. Do not expect success overnight.

Raiding the Garbage Can: This is not an uncommon problem with pigs, dogs, cats, and many other pets. The reasons for it are usually the following: the pet is being underfed, there may be an important ingredient missing from the diet and the pet finds it among the garbage, or the pet has come to know that there are some tasty morsels in the garbage can. Porky knows this because it has watched you throw them in there, or it can smell them. Pigs can, of course, be little shockers at rummaging because their snouts are ideal for flipping lids off the cans and because they simply just love to eat. They can also open cupboard doors and those of a refrigerator.

In the case of garbage cans, the ideal remedy is removal of the reinforcer—the can itself. However, this is not always practical, and in any case it applies only to that particular item. You should ascertain whether or not the quantity and quality of the diet is adequate for the size of your pet. Usually there is not a problem—only an inquisitive and greedy little piglet. Porky is a wise little fellow. When he sees you opening cupboards or the refrigerator, he quickly notes that what comes out often goes into his dinner dish. He knows his meals are kept in these places. Why wait for you if he can open them himself!

Rather than having to barricade the cupboards, the best solution—and one that will be applicable to a number of similar problems—is to firmly implant in your pet's memory that opening these cupboards, stealing from a table, or doing anything that you (not your pet) consider naughty, is associated with an unpleasant consequence.

You could simply say "no" in a firm voice each time you catch the little villain in the act, and this may well prove totally satisfactory. However, the problem with this approach is that for correction of a low-threshold instinct (feeding), it may not be effective all the time. Porky may respond each time you are actually present; but when you are not, there is nothing to offset his strong desire to eat. A stimulus is needed that will be effective regardless of whether or not you are present.

Even though this piglet is very cute, don't let it get away with behavior that will be undesirable as it gets older.

The requirements for this stimulus are—first of all—a lot of patience and then either a bunch of keys, a tin with marbles in it, a throw chain (choke collar as used on dogs), or a water pistol. While you can be present when this negative stimulus is effected, it is always better if you can conceal yourself. When you see your pet attempting to open a cupboard door, you should then throw the keys at it or squirt it with water. This comes as a negative shock to the porcine pilferer—almost like magic emanating from the cupboard or refrigerator door. This practice, which must be repeated as often as possible, is a highly effective remedy.

Once your pet is convinced that every attempt to open the door will result in a nasty surprise, the whole idea becomes altogether less appealing. However, consistency is the keyword to success, as it is with all training. When negative stimuli are to be a remedial tool, always try to implement them without your pet seeing that you are involved. In other words, try to throw the tin can or squirt the water when porky is not watching you.

Biting: This is a habit that must be stopped from the outset because it could get porky and you, as his owner, in an awful lot of trouble and expense—especially in the USA, where people throw big-dollar law suits about like confetti!

Basically, if you have a pig that has become a very aggressive biter, you should refer to more detailed training books because the subject is complex and beyond a few paragraphs. Because biting is such a dangerous habit, you might consider seeking the counsel of a good dog trainer.

There are two types of biting: one is that done accidentally as porky takes food from your hand, and the other is with malice (either through fear, or possessiveness of an object, person, or place). Charging is basically a self-protecting action, even though it appears as aggression. As mentioned before, attack is a good form of defense. This is the situation with pigs and other herd animals that have no intention of eating you!

Let us consider accidental biting first because all animals do it—whether they are birds, puppies, human babies, or piglets. Part of growing up is learning what is and is not acceptable behavior. But to learn you must first commit the crime as it were. A young animal has to learn that its teeth can hurt people. If your piglet nips you when taking food, withdraw your hand promptly, say "ouch" or the like, and withhold the food.

Offer the item again. If piggy again nips, withdraw the food again. Slowly your pet will realize that its teeth are hurting you and will then approach your fingers more cautiously. A bite-free mouthing means porky gets the morsel. Please understand that there is a big difference between teaching a piglet to take an item gently and withholding an item when there is no problem—this is teasing and will encourage the piglet to grab, which is the very thing you do not want to happen.

With regard to porky's biting of non-food items, this habit should be discouraged from the word go. A pet pig that develops this habit has done so only because you have allowed it. If a piglet approaches you and nips (as opposed to a fear bite because you have mishandled it), this action is unacceptable and must be counteracted immediately. A very firm "no" should be adequate with a piglet. If this fails to elicit the required response, then a quick tap on the nose and a "no" at the same time (primary and discriminative reinforcers) are the next level of discipline. Consistency in the use of these methods will help to achieve success. But always remember that

These four friendly piglets are posing for a picture atop a donkey's back.

biting and charging are part of a much wider behavior pattern. They indicate an insecure pet that is fearful. If you alleviate the insecurity, then a fearful pet should never become a problem for you.

THE SIT COMMAND

The sit command is useful for your pet to learn not only because it will be used when you are out walking with porky but also because it is an excellent counter-conditioning aid—your pet cannot be in the sit position and easily nudge you as well. Use a treat at first, and hold it just above piggy's nose, thus causing the head to be raised. After a few times, raise the treat higher. Often, your pet will sit down as it is easier for him to maintain sight of the treat. Praise and reward him, at the same time using the command "sit."

If your pet will willingly stand by your side, this is even better because you can gently press down its rear end while holding the treat above its nose. Once the exercise has been successfully accomplished a few times, you should not offer a treat each time. You are now practicing schedule stretching, and eventually the command and praise alone will be sufficient. If you prefer, you may first teach your pet to walk on a lead as this will mean porky is at your side, whereby the sit exercise may be more easily learned.

LEAD TRAINING

Along with the other basic matters that we have discussed, lead training is the final essential requirement for your little porcine pal. It allows you to take him out in the big world and meet other people, which in itself makes for a more contented and self-confident little piggy. You should never attempt to lead train your pet until it is totally relaxed when you

Teaching a pig to sit on command is not difficult and will help keep it manageable in certain situations.

touch any part of its body. If it is at all nervous before you start on this exercise, you will merely have a panicky pet on the other end of the lead. In this state, no animal—including you—can learn.

Before discussing the procedure, let us consider the objective because it is a matter of some debate within the potbelly pig hobby. Some owners believe the pig should walk just behind the owner while rather more people believe it should be just ahead. This author, along with all who have experience in dog training, prefers to have the pig at the trainer's side—head level with the left knee (or the right if you are left handed).

Controlling your pig is the objective of the exercise. If your pet trails behind you or forges ahead, you have virtually no control over its actions. On a city street, this could be extremely dangerous. If the pet panicked, it could easily move off to one side and entangle its lead around someone's legs or another object, which will increase its state of frenzy. If it is attacked by a dog, you are in no position to do anything. In each of these situations all you can hope to do is to haul in your pet or rapidly move along the lead to reach him.

These reactions are totally undesirable and unnecessary with correct training. Further, only by being in close contact with you can instructions be given to porky and changes in direction be indicated. In the event of a problem, you are situated next to your pet and thus are far more able to totally control events.

First stage: Before any training is attempted, it is important that your pet is quite familiar with its harness. Show it often to porky before ever putting it on. Stroke his body with it. When this has been achieved, you can place the harness on him and let

When purchasing a harness for your pig, make sure it fits properly.

him wear it for a short period. Fuss over him and maybe offer a treat so that he associates the harness with nice things. Do not leave the harness on when you are not present: it could get caught on something, and this will really freak piggy out.

Once your pet is quite happy toddling about in his harness, you can then attach the lead and simply walk him around the house. Do not try at this stage to pull or tug, but slowly let your pet feel the lead trail on his back. You go where porky goes.

Second Stage: Let your pet feel some restraint on the lead, but do not attempt to pull. It is much better to coax your pet to follow where you go by offering a treat. Bit by bit, use a shorter amount of lead until porky can only travel a few feet from you. Now, with a gentle tug and release, you can encourage your pet to catch up if it is behind or slow down if it is ahead. Hold the lead in your right hand, and pat your knee with your left hand in order to encourage porky to come close to you. Again, use a treat (and praise) initially; but once you are getting results, discontinue using the treats and simply use praise.

All early lead-training sessions must be done in a quiet place where there are minimal distractions. It is a good idea to practice lead training in a location that abuts a wall or building because it enables you to restrict the left lateral space in which porky can move. Ultimately, your pet will be by your side but on a loose lead. You will then practice right and left turns. Concentrate on the left turns initially because they are easier for your pet to understand (your leg "helps" to tell porky that you are turning). You may decide to join a dog-training class, but discuss this with the trainer first. You can also purchase a book on training.

Dogs are taught with collars or choke chains and respond well to them. Piglets panic more readily with them so the harness is the better training aid. However, a harness requires more patience because it is not causing physical discomfort (which is the basis of choke-chain training). The main problem with dogs is that they want to rush ahead all of the time, but this is not such a problem with pigs. Porkies get slower and slower with age, a decided advantage for many people that own

A nice quiet area, free of distractions, is the perfect place for a training session.

Let your pig get accustomed to a harness first before attaching a lead.

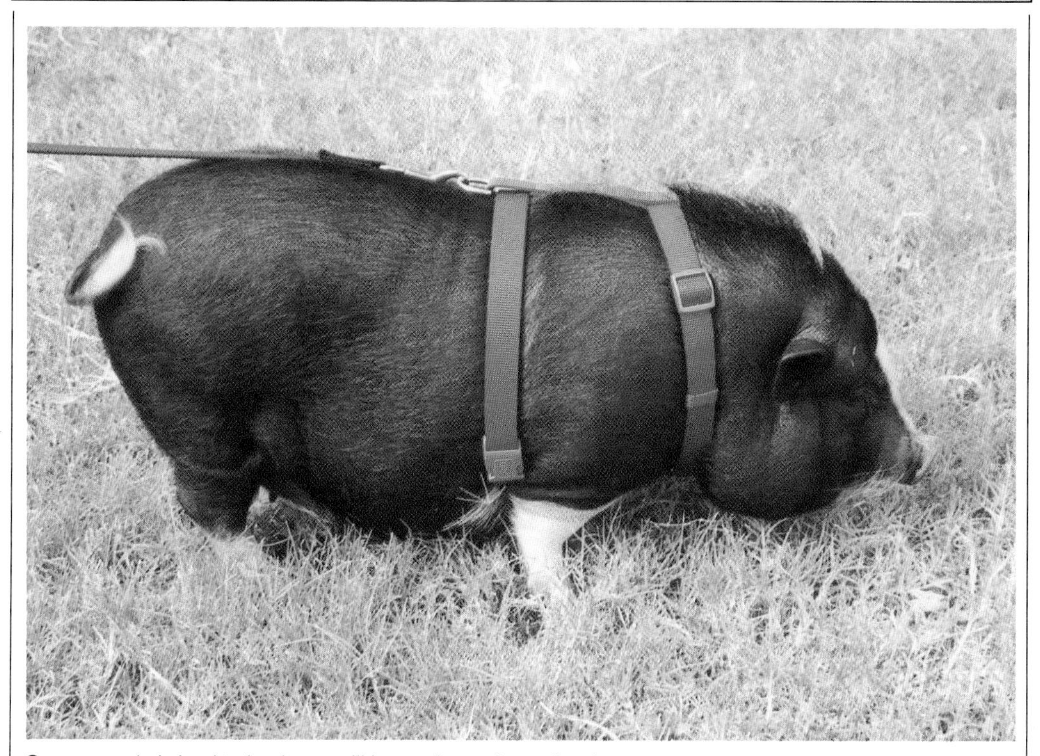

Once your pig is lead trained, you will be ready to take porky about town.

them.

Once your piggy is lead trained, you can take him to more varied places so that he is exposed to a wide variety of situations. A word of caution though: dogs do not eat the environment, but pigs do. Never allow your pet to gobble up flowers or other vegetation from parks or residences as it goes for a stroll with you. If you and porky live in the city, take a pooper scooper with you.

THE SPOILED PIG

Never view your porcine pet through rose-colored glasses. If you do, you will run into problems. More importantly, you may end up with a very dangerous pet. Do not put off training in the hope that porky will get better or will be easier to train as he gets older. This is "cop-out" thinking. An untrained pig will get worse and will be far harder to break from bad habits the older it gets. You would not let your children do as they please so do not let your pet do as it pleases. If you have developed a strong bond of affection with porky, it will not resent your disciplinary actions because they will be minimal—if you started out correctly. All animals receive discipline from their parents and others in their society if they overstep what is regarded as correct. You are replacing your piglet's mother and the pig society that would normally teach the youngster what is acceptable. Never be harsh. Always try to work out the best way to achieve an objective without using punitive methods, but never be so sentimental that you allow porky to be the boss and become a porcine hooligan.

Breeding Considerations and Theory

It is a reality of life that whenever a pet animal becomes very popular, it is not long before a small army of people try to jump on the bandwagon in order to make some fast money. It has to be said that a number of these people do make big profits if they arrive in the market at the right time—when demand far exceeds the supply. Usually, this situation is short-term because these get-rich-quick merchants soon begin to flood the market with poor stock. They then start price cutting in order to make up for lost high-profits-by-volume sales.

The media often make matters worse by implying that all breeders are making big money from these pets. This brings in its wake even more backyard breeders. What then follows is a period of stagnation during which the market is cleansed of these leeches and returns to being a steady-growth market (assuming the bad breeders have not ruined the reputation of the pet in the quest for easy money).

At this time, the potbelly market is still expanding; but the prices now realized for pets is falling because the supply is beginning to catch up with the demand. Quality pigs will still be a worthwhile investment, but even their prices will probably fall in all but a few instances over the next few years. On the other hand, the demand for colored pigs, meaning bicolors, whites, and patterned varieties, will likely be steady to very good when compared to prices for black pigs. It is difficult to forecast how successful the show side of the potbellied pig will be, but I suspect that it will become the backbone of the hobby.

Taking all of these factors into consideration, it can be said that unless you plan to take breeding very seriously, the days of quick high profits are now over. Further, you should identify very carefully that area of the market that appeals to you. You can specialize in supplying quality pets, you may prefer to concentrate your efforts toward developing a good show-winning line, or you may think in terms of being one of the pioneer color-breeders. What is for sure is that if you try to spread your objectives too widely, the chances are high that none of them will be achieved, or only marginally so.

Breeding pigs are not ideal pets, and the requirements for developing a worthwhile herd are many. Do not even think that you can maybe make some good pin money by breeding one or two pet sows: it doesn't work like that. Be prepared to overcome many difficulties, work very long hours at times, and have the needed cash to at least commence your program—without having to make compromises almost from the outset. In this chapter, we will review many aspects of breeding, but do understand that what is discussed is actually only the bare bones of the subject. You should be able to decide from the text if you are sure that you wish to become a breeder. If you are, then you should heed the advice given, and plan the whole operation very carefully—much more so than you did when obtaining your first pet potbelly.

The first point of advice is that you should not attempt to set yourself up as a breeder until you have gained

Before starting a breeding program, make sure that you have the time, space, and money available to do things correctly.

practical experience in keeping a piggie. Such a course of action will either convince you it is to be your only goal in life or it will put you off the whole idea for good! Breeding can be divided into three broad areas: initial considerations and requirements, breeding theory, and practical breeding. Here we will look into the first two and deal with practical breeding in the next chapter.

INITIAL CONSIDERATIONS

Under this heading are included the matters of legalities, space, time, and cost.

Legalities: In many areas, potbellied pigs are not regarded as pets. This means that you may live in a locality that does not allow the breeding of these animals. Even if pets are allowed, breeding may not be. You will need to check what the actual requirements are in your locality for breeding potbellies. The program will probably have to be put on a commercial footing, whereby you will be classified as a farm-pig breeder—thus subject to the usual requirements for swine management. They are more complex than those for pet pigs. You may have to move to another locality if you really want to be a breeder.

Space: While you do not need a great deal of space to accommodate two or three breeding sows, you should plan ahead to the day when your herd increases in numbers. In general, most breeders find that they need far more space than was originally thought. Apart from the actual pig housing, you will need isolation quarters, ample storage facility, and, no doubt, undercover storage for mechanical aids and vehicles. You will also need pasture—just how much depending on the quality of the land available and your own thoughts on how much land you would like to own. Certainly, in excess of two acres would be a desirable state.

Time: Unless you are a very wealthy person, the chances are that your breeding operation will be, at least initially, a part-time venture. Do you have the time to devote to all of the hard work needed to succeed? Think very hard about this matter because piglets take up a lot of time, as do people who will be visiting you in order to see your stock. Further, if you plan to exhibit, this too is a very time-consuming area of the project. Who will look after your stock while you are away at shows?

The Cost: If you thought the cost of your first pet potbelly, together with all of its needed paraphernalia, was high, be prepared to take a few deep breaths when starting up even a small breeding program. Do not fall into the trap of becoming a backyard breeder. These people usually house their stock in a converted shed or its like. They surround this "housing" with a small quantity of chicken wire, which defines the quagmire that purports to be the exercise area and pasture! They are short on equipment and even more short in terms of the stock that they are breeding.

Some localities may not permit the breeding of potbellied pigs. Check first, before spending any money on stock or equipment.

Aim for a well-planned, durable facility. You want accommodations with full services supplied to them. You want sufficient equipment to attend to chores in an efficient manner, and you want to commence with, at the very least, typical sound examples of a potbellied pig. Obviously, it would be nice to have an open checkbook to ensure that your stock was of the highest order, but rarely is this the case. Your objective is to steadily improve your stock as a result of your planned breeding program. However, even typically sound stock will cost a good bit more than will pet-quality stock.

You will not start out with a herd as such, and you do not need to own a boar initially. Instead, you will want two nice sows (as unrelated as possible) to commence with if you wish to reduce the risk that a single sow proved not to be what was expected of her. You can indeed begin with just one sow, but initial progress will be very slow. Conversely, it is not wise to start with too many. You do not want to find yourself overburdened in upkeep and time aspects while you are feeling your way into the program. Plan your budget prudently, but realistically, to ensure that you have the cash to get underway. Bear in mind that expenses for feed, the vet, advertising, and maybe exhibition will have to be met before you get any returns on your surplus stock.

The consequences of under-capitalization apply as equally to a part-time breeding program as they do to any full-fledged business, so do your financial homework carefully. Do not get underway until you are sure you can afford it. This might mean

When selecting breeding stock, only good quality specimens should be considered.

obtaining your accommodations the first year and your stock the next, which is better than compromising on both.

BREEDING THEORY

The basis of breeding theory revolves around the subject of genetics. This is well beyond the scope of this book. This said, a broad overview of its importance to a breeder is worthwhile because it has direct influence on both your breeding strategy and on the stock that you initially select. Many hobbyists who cannot be bothered to study the subject will state that for centuries before genetics was even known about, breeders were producing good pigs and developing various breeds of them.

This does not negate the importance of the subject to the modern breeder. To the contrary, it allows him to make more rapid progress than was the case in the past. The breeders of yesteryear who were successful may not have understood the subject, but they were using its principles. You can avoid many pitfalls by knowing how the units of inheritance—chromosomes and the genes on them—pass features from one generation to the next. Such a knowledge by no means ensures that you will produce better pigs because so many other factors are involved in breeding. The subject is thus another tool—a very important one—in your kit of those things that will increase your chances of success if you can use them judiciously. It will be almost obligatory knowledge to those who wish to specialize in breeding present and future new colors. However, even if you do not study genetics as a subject, it is hoped that the general nature of what follows will alert you to many aspects of breeding theory that will be of benefit to you both before, and after, you actually obtain breeding stock.

SELECTING STOCK

The appearance of a pig is created

An understanding of genetics will help a breeder in the selection, pairing, and breeding of potbellied pigs.

by the combined action of all of the genes that it inherits from its parents. While color is a relatively easy feature to work with from a genetic standpoint, the same is not true of conformation. Colors in potbellies are the result of gene mutations. As such, they are relatively easily manipulated because they are inherited in a number of very predictable ways that can be monitored. Any relationship between them and body structure is, at the very best, loose. Normally, there is no such relationship: the structural quality of a pig and its color can be regarded as totally separate entities.

However, body structure is not genetically simple because all aspects of it are interrelated. Because it is not dependent on mutations it cannot be written down—as can color—in genetic formulas. This makes it very difficult to evaluate the worth of a given pig purely on the basis of its appearance. Some genes are known as dominant in their action, which means they express themselves when in single dose. Others are recessive, which means they must be present in double dose in order to be expressive. Others express themselves on a build-up basis, meaning that the more of them there are the more movement there is toward an extreme of a given feature (such as back length or shortness). Finally, there are others that are incompletely dominant or recessive. All of this makes for great complexity. Let us consider a hypothetical example to show how things work in what is regarded as a desirable feature.

There will be a potential genetic range for a feature: from that which is desired to that which is the unwanted extreme. Let us use a pig's back length as an example. A pig may look perfect for its back length, but it may be carrying genes for extreme shortness or extreme length, or for both. But, for one reason or another, they are not able to express themselves in this pig. By random chance, this situation may also hold true for other features of this same pig.

When it is paired to another pig that also might have gained its appearance via the same chance route, it is quite possible that the genes for extremes of a given feature will be received from both parents. The result is some piglets with overly long backs or with backs that are too short, depending on the chance way the genes in the "pool" of the parents combine. The piglets' appearance is hardly what was anticipated from the appearance of the parents and would no doubt surprise and frustrate the breeder.

There may, of course, also be some offspring with the desired back length. Other apparent virtues in both parents may likewise break up in their offspring so that the entire litter of piglets is little more than an assemblage of mediocre specimens. Those that have nice back length might have other features that have badly deteriorated compared to those seen in their parents.

Now, another pair of pigs, which do not look quite as nice as the pair just discussed—thus are never likely to win beauty prizes—may be sound rather than eye catching. They may have obtained their appearance via a totally different route. When their ancestors were bred, any offspring that displayed short or long backs were culled, thus never bred from. With the passage of a number of generations, all genes involved in the creation of long or short backs were removed and replaced by those for average (in this case, desirable) length.

This pair, in theory, could never produce long- or short-backed offspring. So why are they not as good looking as the other pair of pigs? The answer is that their legs may be shorter or longer in ratio to their back length, or their heads may be larger or smaller. These qualities will clearly affect what we perceive as being the entire pig. Given enough generations and assuming careful selection of the breeding stock, there would come a time when the offspring that originated from these pigs would match the all-around excellence of the first pair of pigs discussed. As such, they would be far superior pigs from a breeding viewpoint because they had no undesirable genes in their make-up (genotype). All litters would be to a consistently high standard—a state of idealism will have been attained.

To reach such a state, there are other requirements. Firstly, it would be essential that all inferior stock is removed by the selection process at each generation, which assumes the breeder is capable of making such decisions. Secondly, it would obviously be critical that any pigs introduced to

If you do not know the genetic background of a pig, it will be through trial and error that you will determine if it is a good producer of quality young.

the breeding line have a similar purity of genes for the features under consideration. If they did not, then such features would deteriorate, at least for a few generations while the negative qualities were bred out.

In reality, no one ever reaches a state of idealism because of the very fact that beautiful conformation is a perceived state. It is not only subject to the whims of judges and breeders but also so complex that it would be all but impossible to bring the desired genes together and totally exclude those regarded as undesirable. For this to be done, we would need to fully understand the genotype of every feature and of every gene linkage in the species. It would also mean that the breeder would need to maintain a herd the size of which would not be a practical proposition to any but a funded research institute.

Breeding for color is fine, but soundess should be your first concern.

A potbelly breeder is also faced with another very important problem. Two extremely attractive and well-bred pigs may be of different sizes. Both may be pure in their breeding, so it might seem a good idea to pair them. However, the genes that created the smaller pig's back length (and all of the other features that make it a super pig) will, of course, represent a different part of the range potential for these features when compared with the larger pig. When the two are brought together, the result will be total genetic disharmony. The offspring will in all probability not possess many of their parents' virtues. The recombination of genes might destroy the ratios of one body part to another that made each parent such an outstanding pig.

Thus, planned breeding is all about removing undesired genes and replacing them with desirable ones. Another way of saying this is that it is a system that aims to reduce all variables. When selecting stock, the more you know about every animal in a pig's pedigree the better you are able to assess a potential boar or sow's worth. More important still is the fact that you should be acquainted with the known problems in a given line and how consistent the line is in producing its features. Ultimately, it comes down to knowing just how good a breeder is. This is determined by the selection standards he is known to follow. Clearly, any breeder who maintains detailed breeding records and has an accepted record of success will not be able to sell you breeding stock at a price that would compare with that of a breeder who mates any pig to any pig and hopes to get one or two good specimens upon which he can build his reputation.

When you purchase your first sow(s), it is most unlikely that you will have been able to conduct an in-depth study of breeding lines that are available, and at this stage in the breed's development you might not have too much material to work with anyway. This being the case, use a pragmatic definition of what constitutes a good breeder: one who is considered by a competent authority to

Detailed records of your breeding efforts are important. They will help determine the better breeding pigs and possible breeding results.

be knowledgeable in the field of potbellied pig husbandry. Visit shows, and talk to as many people as you can. Look at their stock, and request to see their breeding records to see if they are kept in a detailed manner.

The matter of the importance of a boar is not related to the notion that he has any more influence over quality than does the sow. A sow can be as prepotent as a boar for her virtues. Both parents contribute 50% of their genes to each litter—never more, or less, than this percent. The singular reason the boar is so important is because he has a far greater opportunity to spread his genes throughout a population than does the sow. She is limited to probably two litters per year as an average, whereas a boar can certainly sire many dozens if he is regarded as being something special.

This brings us to another consideration in breeding. Having established that quality can be more implied than real, the wise breeder selects a boar based on proven quality, rather than on that which is assumed. In animal species for which there is a hard-and-fast measure for quality, this is not a problem. For example, if you wish to breed a racing mare, you will select a stallion that has proven its ability to run fast. Additionally, you will want to know that it has sired many fast-running offspring, thus proving that its ability is not just "heart" but genetic as well. When a pig or cow breeder selects breeding stock that is to produce offspring with good yield potential, be this in meat or milk, he uses only stock that has a proven record for this quality. With a pet or show animal, the measure used is more abstract and based on opinion (the owner or a judge) rather than on real measurables.

This situation means that many pet breeders (in the widest sense, thus

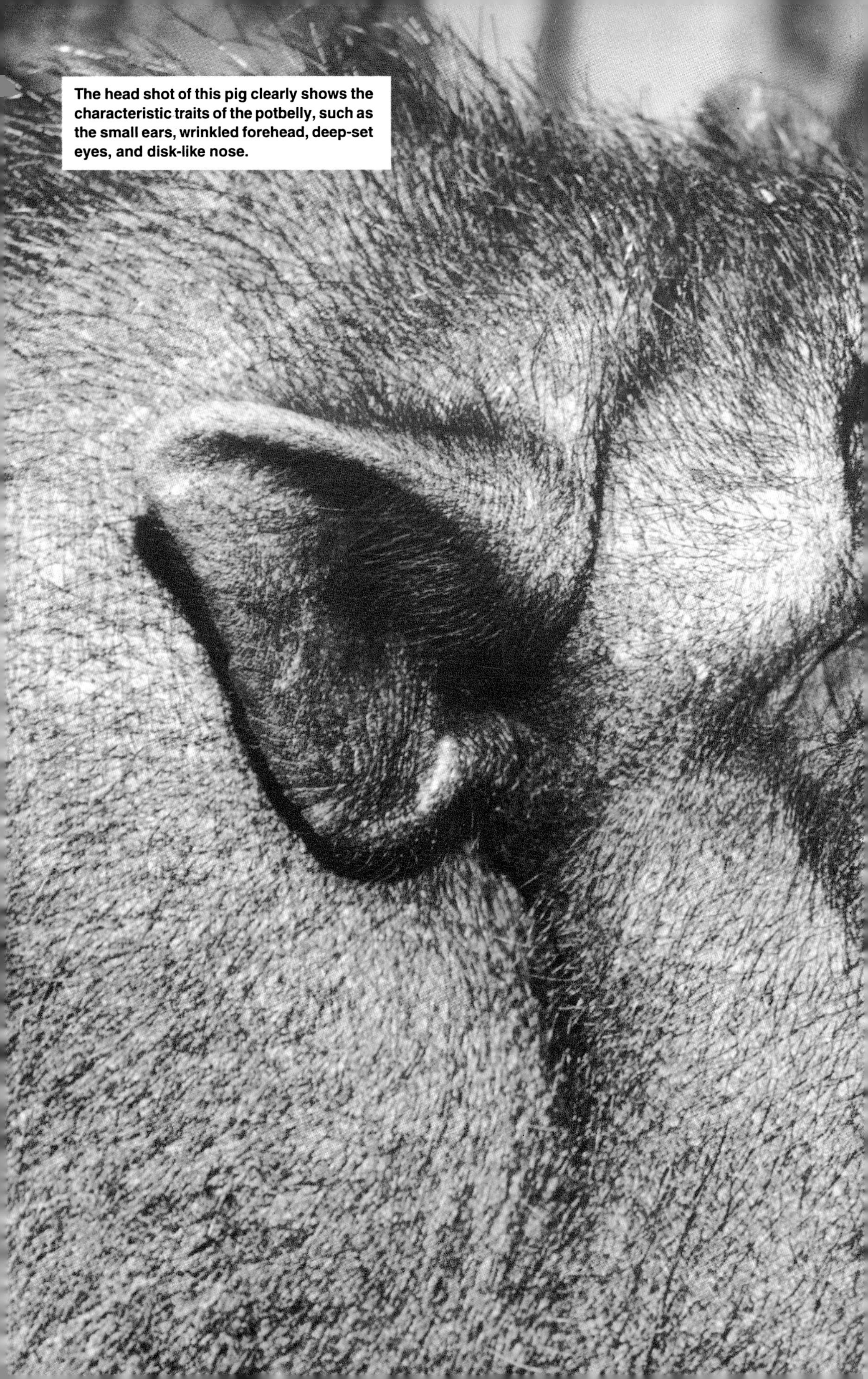

The head shot of this pig clearly shows the characteristic traits of the potbelly, such as the small ears, wrinkled forehead, deep-set eyes, and disk-like nose.

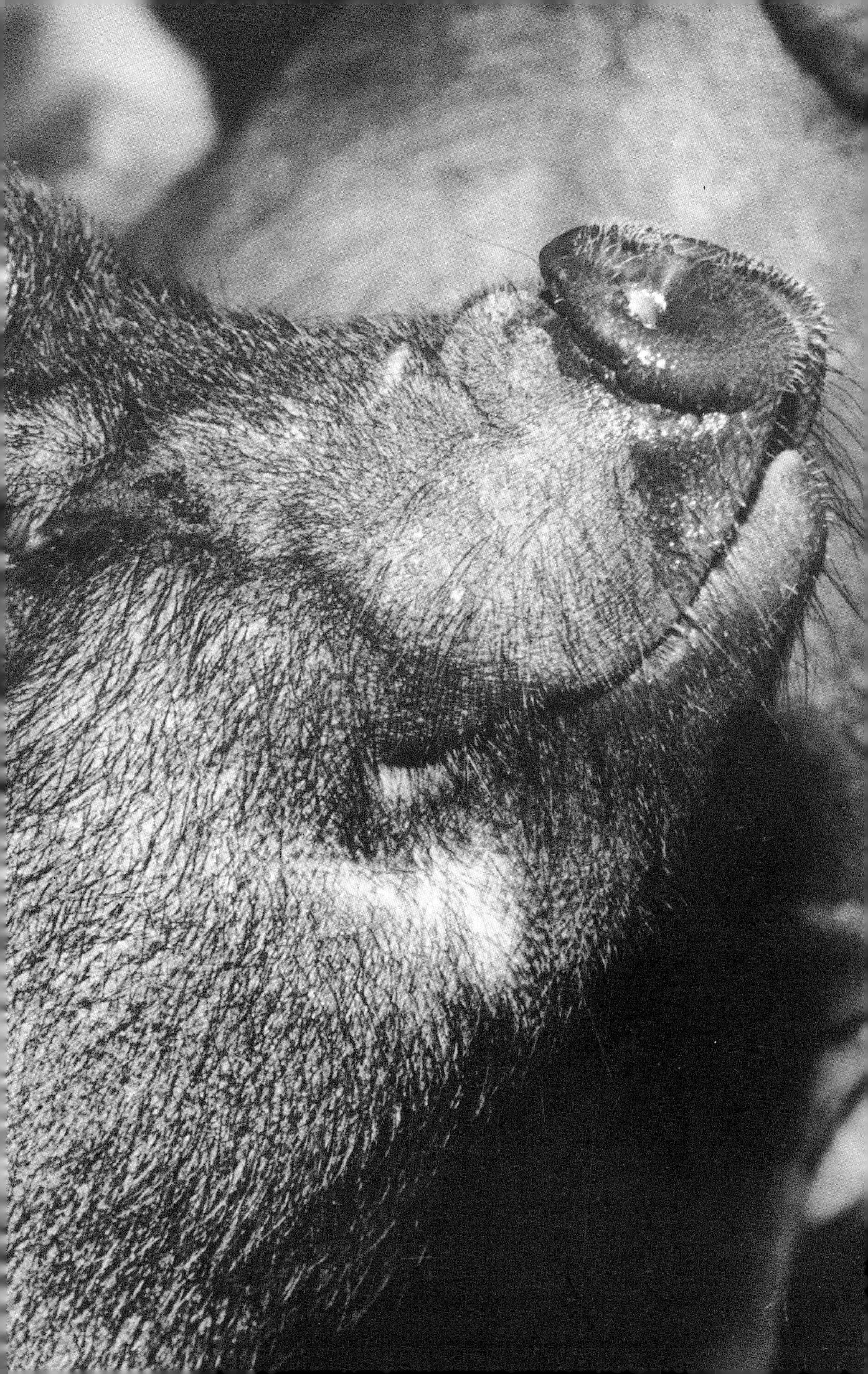

including those producing show specimens) get carried away with unproven virtues. That this is so is easily seen by the number of top-winning examples that are used for breeding simply because they are the current big winners, rather than because they have proven anything in a breeding sense or because the owners of the female animals to be bred have done worthwhile research into the breeding suitability of the male animals. If the true record of many so-called outstanding males in various pet species were to be carefully analyzed, it would be found that they actually contributed very little to their breeds. The fact that they may have produced many winners proves little in itself. When studying the worth of any sire, all facts must be taken into account. For example, the success of the winners they have produced might be a better reflection on the quality of certain of their mates than of themselves. Additionally, if the number of their winning offspring was converted into a percentage of all of the stock that they had sired, their record might pale in comparison to that of a much less known individual with a far superior record of siring high-quality stock. (This assumes that both were paired to a random selection of females of different quality so that such a comparison was valid.)

Personality, as well as soundness, is a very important part of a pig's overall attractivness.

Never overrate a boar because it is a winner or underrate the importance of the sow in being equally responsible for producing superior stock. Again, at this time in potbellied pigs, you cannot really judge which boars will prove to have stamped their qualities on the breed because enough generations have not yet passed. Nonetheless, all of this knowledge is of value to you because it broadens your perspective of what will be happening as you develop in this hobby and of what data you should be trying to compile for future use in your program.

DISPOSITION AND HEALTH

Two features of superior pet and show stock that are often overlooked, or at least compromised, in breeding programs are those of disposition and health. They should be the most important considerations of the program. That this is not always the case is seen in all pets in which problems related to character and health are well documented. It can be evident in dogs that have a bad reputation for their aggressive or unreliable natures. It can be evident in a cage bird that is unable to care for its own chicks (necessitating that the eggs be fostered), or because the fecundity or survival rate in a breed has become so low that it has become a major concern.

These situations can happen only when breeders choose to continue breeding with stock that looks good but has a definite problem with disposition and/or health. Often the breeders are not forthcoming with data on these matters because it would decrease the value of their stock. If, as this author forecasts, the show side of the potbellied hobby becomes the only

Pigs that will be used for breeding will not make ideal pets. They may become less agreeable and often lose much of their housebreaking training.

means used to determine quality, the sad but hard reality will be that disposition and health will be problem features as the future unfurls.

If a breeder has a winning pig of great beauty but finds it is having many health problems, and is producing stock that is likewise lacking in vigor, or has dubious natures, the quest for fame and money may override the fact that the pig in question should be removed from the breeding program.

It must be said that it is far easier and more profitable to develop a show-winning line of pigs if character and health aspects are taken out of the equation. If either of these aspects are overlooked, it will result in negative characteristics. They will be considered poor specimens to own because of possible health problems, and lack of positive pet attributes. But if you care for the future of the hobby and for the many piglets that you will sell as pets, it behooves you to put character and health priorities ahead of beauty. It is not difficult to monitor health problems, but character is very difficult to assess because it is so dependent on environmental factors.

BREEDING METHODS

Having given you ample food for thought on many topics that you should apply your mind to, there is then the question of what breeding methods are open to you. Having gone to the trouble of obtaining stock that you feel meets your idea of being sound, you will be trying to maintain or improve on its qualities over future generations. There have been many volumes of text devoted to breeding methods, and you are advised to avail yourself of them. They should be books devoted to breeding theory rather than books that are of a general-care type. You will not find such books devoted to potbellied pigs at this time, but any work on pig breeding or on cattle, dogs, or horses will be just fine. The theory aspect of breeding applies to all animals.

Here we can end the chapter by briefly commenting on the three basic methods that can form part of any breeding program.

Inbreeding: This is best defined as the breeding of individuals that are more closely related to each other than is the average relationship of the population. It is more commonly held as being the mating of individuals that are very closely related, such as father to daughter, mother to son, or brother to sister. Inbreeding is strongly associated with negatives. This is not because the method in itself creates problems—at least not at the level likely to be practiced by most breeders—but because the individuals used carry problems. It is important that this distinction is understood. If a problem gene, be it for an undesirable feature or for a major health problem, is not within the genotype of two breeding animals, then no matter how long continued inbreeding was practiced within subsequent generations, the fault or the health problem would not be a feature of that line.

This piglet is definitely too young to be taken from its mother, but will be ready to go when about six to eight weeks of age.

Inbreeding thus increases the chances of highlighting problems because it increases the chances that hidden faults will be brought to the surface. This is a benefit and is why many breeding lines were carefully inbred initially to achieve the dual objective of fixing in virtues while at the same time highlighting problems. The down side of close inbreeding is that if the desired feature happens to be genetically linked to an undesirable feature, the latter also becomes fixed.

On the basis of evidence in numerous species, it would seem that continued inbreeding will result in problems in the form of reduced litter numbers, reduced body weight of infants, increased infant mortality, increased nervousness, and other undesirable aspects. The pig appears to be especially prone to the negative consequences of inbreeding, so it is a method that should be used with care. This is even more important given the very limited pool that today's pet and show stock has been derived from, virtually all of which are being inbred to a greater or lesser degree. A further comment on inbreeding is that it is often thought that it will reduce variability in a line. In other words, it will make for greater pureness of the stock. This is untrue because it may actually increase the variability. If two animals have the genotypes of AA and aa, their offspring will all have the genotype of Aa, which neither of their parents had. If these individuals are paired, the next generation may have any of the following genotypes: AA, Aa, or aa. In other words, variability has increased because Aa is now present in the line.

Only by removing aa (assuming that this is the undesired state) at every generation will you eventually arrive at a stage where only AA and Aa examples are found. Providing you can establish which individuals are AA, you can eventually reach the time when all the stock is AA and thus pure. The key factor is not inbreeding per se but inbreeding combined with rigorous selection at every generation.

In order for pigs to raise healthy young, proper diet and housing are necessary.

Linebreeding: This is a dilute form of inbreeding and is the most popular method of developing a line of stock. The basis of this method is that if one or two pigs are selected that are regarded as being especially outstanding, by the careful use of them and their progeny, it is possible to raise the incidence of their desired features (genes) in the line in question. The benefit of linebreeding is that being less intense, there is a reduced risk that unwanted features will manifest themselves. At the same time, there is greater flexibility to remove faults and to add virtues. So, all in all, it represents a very sound way to steadily improve stock.

Random Breeding: This method is very typical of many breeders' systems if a study of their matings was to be carefully conducted. By definition, random breeding might well include a degree of inbreeding because the basis is that one pursues a policy of selecting stock for certain features without consideration of whether one is trying to bring together an assemblage of similar genes.

The benefits of the method are that certain traits, such as breeding vigor, will not be adversely affected. At the same time, the very random nature of chance is such that outstanding animals are occasionally produced. The down side is that such animals rarely prove to be of any great value in a breeding program. This will not be of any consequence to a person who breeds on a random basis anyway.

Whatever breeding policy you pursue, the effectiveness of the program will only be seen over relatively large numbers of offspring, so progress will reflect how many pigs are within the breeding pool. If you have only one sow, and retain only one of her offspring, it will clearly take a long while before you could hope to achieve any obvious results. The average breeder is invariably a random breeder even though he may claim to be linebreeding.

Even though you may never aspire to own a herd of potbellied pigs, you can only gain from having an insight into breeding theory. You will appreciate what quality stock is all about. You will be less inclined to purchase sows or utilize the services of boars without asking at least some questions of yourself as to what their true breeding merits are or even if they have any. That represents progress and makes for a better breeder.

Breeding Practice

There is no doubt that breeding your pigs represents the height of excitement in the care and management of them. The feeling of achievement is such that it is almost as though you, rather than the sow, had given birth to the piglets! While no pet can really be called "easy" to breed—problems can occur—what can be said with certainty is that pigs are not among those pets that could be regarded as being simple or straightforward to breed.

Once a sow has given birth to a litter (in pigs, the process is known as farrowing), there are many obstacles to overcome before the little piglets are independent of their mother and ready to go to a new home. The death rate of piglets is high in comparison to that seen in many other pets. This is due to a number of causes. Sows, while being protective mothers, cannot be said to be the most caring. In the absence of farrowing pens, many piglets die from being crushed against their housing's walls by their mothers. Sows do not aid their offspring during the birth process, and sows may have difficulty in providing enough milk for their babies.

If a piglet wanders too far from its mother, she will neither carry it back to its nest, as will dogs or cats, nor will she show the same high degree of concern for the piglets that a mare or cow will show for their offspring. Environmental conditions are also critical in pig breeding. All of these facts mean that you, as a breeder, must take a very concerned and active interest in the welfare of your sows and especially of the piglets.

Assuming you have given plenty of thought to the theoretical aspects of breeding and have prepared quality accommodations for your stock, we can now look at the practical aspects, from the choice of the sow, to the breeding process, to the point where the piglets are sold and go to their new homes.

THE BREEDING SOW

A female pig that has never been bred before is known as a gilt. A bred gilt is a female who is pregnant with her first litter. Once a female is one or more years of age, she is called a sow. When selecting breeding stock, your first question may well be "How old should the female be?" The two factors that will influence this choice will be price and quality. A piglet under the age of 12 weeks will be the cheapest option, but you will have to wait a few months before you can breed such a pig. This, of course, means upkeep costs. Further, at such a young age, you cannot say for sure just how nice she will become upon maturity. However, an older gilt whose quality is more obvious will be more costly. Likewise, a young, proven bred female will be even more costly; such a pig is clearly the favored choice because many of the variables have been eliminated. Yet another choice would be to purchase a bred gilt as this is the quickest way to get underway as a breeder. However, it eliminates your ability to select the boar of your choice. The recommended course, if a proven female is beyond your purse limits, would be to select a 4- to 8-month old gilt.

She should obviously be very healthy and conform to the standard for these pets. In particular, look at the following:

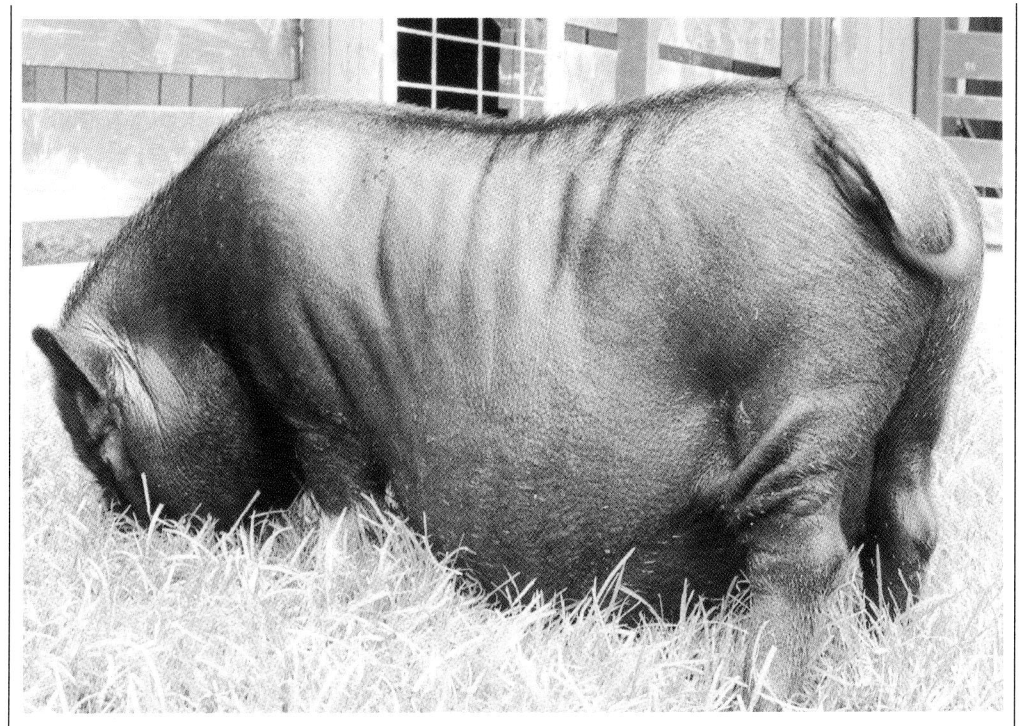

Sows must be in top physical condition before breeding. This will reduce the chances of any problems occuring during pregnancy and farrowing.

1. Watch that she moves very freely. Any hint of lameness is undesirable. If the seller says she has sprained her foot or leg, and if you really like her, you can go back a week or so later and inspect her again. Always place your judgment only in what you see in front of you, not in what you are told about why a feature is not as it should be.

2. View the female from the front, back, sides, and above. The legs viewed from front or back should be straight. The rear legs, in profile, will incline slightly (never excessively) in the pasterns. The hoofs should be compact and undamaged. The back should be nicely dipped but not to the point that it looks excessive. The potbelly should be well formed but should not touch the floor. The tail must be straight, and its root should be high on the rump.

3. The vulva should not be upturned, too small, or too large.

4. Check the underbelly to see that the gilt has at least five pairs of well-formed nipples. If any are rather flat or inverted, they will probably not function well, apart from which their cause may be genetic. You do not want to risk starting with such defects. It is very desirable that you can see the dam (and maybe at least a photo of the sire) of the gilt in front of you as this will give obvious indications of what your gilt will mature to look like in her size and conformation. Inspect the breeding records of the parents. You can by all means ask how good the mother is as a mother, but unless the breeder is unusually honest, this type of question is hardly likely to be answered in other than a positive manner. The question of disposition is always a tricky one, but, even so, try to evaluate the temperament of

the seller's other stock. If they seem nervous, you have to try and make a judgment. Is such a disposition inherent in the stock or is it the result of poor socialization or other environmental factors? Essentially, the stock should not be nervous for either reason, and you will be taking a gamble if your purchase a pig from such stock. Although gilts are normally sold with no guarantees as to their breeding ability, you would be wise to obtain some sort of guarantee that the chosen female will not be infertile. This is obviously very important if you are paying a good price. Some arrangements should be made whereby you can return the gilt and get a refund, or another female, assuming it is firmly established that the female cannot produce offspring. This would be most unlikely but is not unknown. Finally, do check that the gilt does have a permanent identification (tattoo, ear tag, or microchip implant) on her and that all of her papers (pedigree and registration) are in order. You will, of course, also want a written bill of sale and any documentation (vaccination certificates, etc.) that will be required when she is transported to your home. When you get her home, have your vet inspect her at the earliest opportunity.

BREEDING CONDITION

It would be unwise to breed any gilt until she is about 8 months old. Even at this age, she is well short of full physical maturity (which is attained between 12 to 18 months of age). The fact that the female may be biologically capable of breeding at an earlier age does not mean that it is therefore wise that she does so. Some breeders will allow their sows to mate when they are six months of age—with seemingly no ill effects. However, it will not be until later in life that the effects of such an early breeding will begin to show themselves in litter size, reduced offspring vigor, and the like. As far as I know, there have been no long-term studies made on the effects of early breeding in potbellied pigs, so this advice is based on the effects documented in other pets. However, the health condition of the gilt at the time of mating and her subsequent care are probably just as important as her age. Some females are more mature for their age than are others, which is why I would add an extra couple of months—just to be on the safe side.

A most critical factor in pig breeding is that the gilt should not be overweight,as this will create a number of problems. She may have greater difficulty in conceiving, more problems when giving birth to her offspring, will normally lactate poorly (maybe not at all), and may have a reduced litter size. It must be remembered that unlike the boar, whose sole role in reproduction is merely to implant his sperm in the sow, the female has an ongoing relationship with her offspring.

From the moment of

When selecting a breeding sow, obtain as much information as possible about her parents and previous offspring before making any purchasing decisions.

When pregnant, a potbelly pig's stomach may extend so that it touches the ground.

fertilization, their development will be influenced by her physical state via her blood. Any problems that she has may well be transmitted to her babies, which is why it is so critical that she be in the peak of fitness at the onset of breeding. If she is recovering from an illness or already has one, she should not be mated. She should be free of parasites, and her vaccinations should be up to date. If all of these conditions pertain, she can be said to be in fine breeding condition.

Although the boar has no post-mating influence over his offspring, this does not mean that he can be a flabby overweight specimen. Of course, his physical state will have no effect on the features he passes to his offspring, but it may well affect his ability to mate successfully and will determine the litter size. For these reasons, he should be in the same kind of condition as that of his breeding partner.

PLANNING THE MATING

Aspects of selecting a suitable mate for your sow have already been discussed. It is therefore a case of booking the services of the chosen male. You may wish to give thought to a backup boar just in case your first choice should by chance happen to become ill or be injured.

Whether you take the boar to the sow, or vice versa, is really a matter of convenience (distance and cost) rather than of any other consideration. In herd situations, the boar would go to the sow if a number of females are to be mated; but for individual matings, the reverse is normally the order of the day. You can make your arrangements after discussion with the boar's owner, at which time the stud fee should be agreed upon. Once again, if you take the sow to the boar, do not overlook the necessary travel documentation if crossing state lines.

An alternative to direct-contact mating is artificial insemination. It gives you a potentially wider choice of boars and possibly less risk of infection as a result of movement and contact. Such a service is available for potbellied pigs. You can discuss this matter with your vet and the chosen service owners.

BREEDING FACTS

Litter Size: The range in litter size can be anywhere from 1 to 12 but is typically 4 to 8. Although a sow could have more than two litters per year, this is not advisable. Pregnancy and piglet rearing make tremendous demands upon the body of the sow, who should be given ample time to recover after each litter. If this is not done, the result will be a run-down sow that will have smaller and more sickly litters in the future. Your objective is to always produce strong quality piglets, not simply as many of them as you can, which would indicate the only concern was making money rather than balancing financial gain with consideration for the babies and their mother.

A boar, of course, is a different matter and can sire many litters in a year with no adverse effects on his health. But even he should not be expected to work like a machine to the point that his overall stamina is placed at risk. If overused, he may not proceed with the same enthusiasm as a boar whose matings have been spaced so that his reproductive urge remains strong. If a boar is used to service a number of females, bear in mind that he should not be mated to more than, say, two a day over any short period. The consequence of overuse, apart from his lack of enthusiasm, is that the litter size may be reduced due to the drain on his sperm reserves.

Estrus Cycle: The period of time when a female releases eggs for fertilization is known as the estrus cycle, or more commonly the heat. It is the period when the female becomes sexually excited and is prepared to allow herself to be mated. Prior to her coming into heat, the female may mount other females and will tend to urinate more frequently. During this time, her nature may

This average litter of eight piglets will depend on their mother for milk for almost six weeks.

change dramatically. She may become more aggressive, less predictable, and will probably forget any of her training (including litterbox). This is why an unspayed female does not make a good pet. The degree of change in disposition can vary considerably. The pig's estrus cycle occurs every 19 to 23 days and is of 1 to 5 days in duration.

The female is best mated about 24 hours after she is detected as being in heat. This should ensure that the maximum number of sperm are in her oviduct when she begins to ovulate (release eggs for fertilization).

If a female is mated too soon or too late, this will tend to reduce the conception rate, thus the litter size. To detect whether the female is in heat, apply pressure to her back, whereupon she should stiffen up and stand solid, while stiffening her ears. The boar should be present nearby. If she does not stand solid, she is not in heat. Her vulva will be swollen, and there may be a reddish discharge from it. You can test her two or three times a day if possible. Let her be mated 12 and 24 hours after the heat is evident. If a female will "stand" for a boar on more than three successive days, the chances of her conceiving fall dramatically, so further matings at that particular heat are not advised. Some females may have a reduced heat period that lasts for only a couple of days. If this is found to be a feature of your pig's estrus, it is best to mate her as soon as the heat is established.

Gestation Period: This is the time lapse between the fertilization of the ova (eggs) and the birth of the piglets. In pigs, it ranges from 106 to 116 days, with 110 being about the normal average. Pigs born toward the extremes of the range will usually be stillborn (dead at birth) or have problems. The first 30 days after fertilization are very critical. By this time, virtually all physical features of the developing fetus have been formed.

The boar will show considerable interest in the female when she comes into heat.

Pregnancy Detection: Pregnancy can be determined with about a 95% accuracy rate by ultrasonic detection if the procedure is performed in the range of 30 to 45 days after the mating. Beyond the optimum date, the method is less reliable. As the pregnancy progresses, the female will gain weight, which can, of course, confirm pregnancy. If no detection methods are used (there are others apart from that just mentioned) and

When the female stands for the boar with no resistence, she is ready for mating.

It is important to check that a female pig has five sets of fully formed teats before breeding. If any are absent or malformed, it could mean problems in properly feeding her piglets.

the sow is carrying a small litter, it will be more difficult to ascertain pregnancy.

Weaning: This is the period when the piglets are able to begin eating solid foods and no longer rely solely on their mother's milk. In potbellies, it will normally occur when they are four to seven weeks of age. The mother pig will come back into estrus anywhere from three to eight days after she has weaned her offspring. However, as the weaning period is variable, it is quite possible that she may come into estrus while nursing her babies.

When it comes to the weaning period, try to allow it to be as natural as possible. Do not attempt to wean piglets prematurely (four weeks or under) in the hopes that it will make for better imprinting on humans. This is a very debatable subject with other pets as well: dogs, cats, and large parrots. However, what evidence there is suggests that in pigs, premature weaning is linked to nervous aggression later in life.

ENVIRONMENTAL CONDITIONS

In order to maximize on both the size of the litter and the number of piglets that survive to weaning age, it is critical that environmental conditions be at their best. Each female should have her own pen, and the ambient temperature of the building she is housed in should be controlled. In her own pen, you can carefully monitor the feeding regimen, which is not possible if two or more sows share a pen. If a pen is shared, the sow at the top of the hierarchy will eat her own share of food and part of that of others in the pen. Thus, one sow will become overweight while the others are short on rations. Apart from this imbalance, females in direct contact with each other might raise the stress level in all of them as the pregnancy progresses. Fighting could break out, and this could result not only in embryonic damage to some of the developing fetuses but also could create the risk of infection from any lesions created.

Temperature has a dramatic effect on all aspects of porcine reproduction. If it rises above 85 degrees, this stresses pigs, and the litter size may be reduced by up to 40 per cent as a result of prenatal embryonic death. Changes in humidity, together with the number of hours of daylight, will also influence embryonic development. In the case of the boar, high temperatures, as well as sudden temperature changes over a short period of time, will reduce sperm production dramatically. With these facts in mind, it is therefore prudent to ensure that a thermostatic cooling system is operative during summer-month breedings, when heat and humidity are likely to be factors.

VACCINATIONS

In order to ensure that the embryos have the best possible chance to survive in good health, females that are to be bred should be vaccinated against leptospirosis, parvovirus, and erysipelas six weeks before being bred and again three weeks later. They should receive immunity against *Escherichia coli* about 45 days prior to farrowing, and this should be repeated 24 days later. You can treat against mange with injections, and you should deworm the sow three weeks before farrowing. A breeding sow is required by state law to be tested periodically (check with your vet) for pseudorabies and brucellosis. The boar should likewise be protected against the major diseases and parasites before being used for breeding.

BREEDING AND NUTRITION

Because of the harmful effects of overweight in a female that has been bred, care must be taken with the diet. During the early part of the gestation period, food intake can be increased slightly to ensure that the developing embryos receive sufficient nutrients.

However, this only applies if the female is in hard breeding condition. In the last few days before farrowing, the diet can be reduced slightly to remove the risk of excess food accumulating in the digestive tract and creating unwanted bulk and digestive disorders. Once the piglets are born, the female's rations should be increased to accommodate the extra needs of nursing. By the time the piglets are two to four weeks old,

It should be seen that the sow gets fed properly when feeding piglets to assure that there is enough milk produced for all.

A farrowing encloser can be purchased or you can build one yourself.

the female should be eating about twice her normal non-breeding-state rations. Thereafter, the feed can steadily be reduced back to normal so as to reduce the milk flow. Throughout the gestation period, the female should be allowed to exercise so that she remains very fit.

THE BIRTH PROCESS

On the day of farrowing, the female should not be given solid foods, but access to water should be maintained. Pigs can be farrowed either in a special farrowing pen or in their regular housing. A farrowing pen can be purchased. It consists of a central metal pen with smaller pens on either side for the piglets to move into, thus preventing the risk of being crushed by the mother when she lays down. Infrared lamps can be suspended over the piglets' quarters to provide the vital heat needed by young porkies. Farrowing pens are fitted with butt plates, which allow the piglets to move from one side of the pen to the other in order to feed from mom—whichever way she is positioned. The pen can be lined with wood shavings and hay.

A heat lamp is suggested so that young piglets get the heat needed to stay warm and healthy.

If the female farrows in her regular housing, be sure she is supplied with ample nesting material so that she can make a nest. If she is not given nesting material, she may get frustrated, thus stressed.

The farrowing period is very variable. It may be over in as little as an hour or so or may take up to eight hours, depending on the female and the number of piglets that she has. The time between births is equally varied: it can range from a few minutes to one or more hours. Typically, it will be 15-20 minutes. As each piglet is born, the umbilical cord normally severs of itself. If it does not, you will need to assist because pigs do not sever this lifeline as do dogs, cats, and many other mammals. Likewise, the fetal membrane that encases the newborn will normally break so that the piglet can breathe. If it does not, you must sever it with your fingers; otherwise, the piglet may suffocate. Once this has been attended to, you can then cut the cord if it has not severed.

Tie a piece of cotton thread (after dipping it in antiseptic) around the cord about an inch or so from the piglet's navel. Now the cord can be cut on its placental end. The cord attached to the piglet should be dabbed with iodine to prevent infection. It will shrivel up over the next day or so.

If a piglet appears lifeless, do not assume it is dead. Give it a very brisk

An ample amount of nesting material should be supplied for the expecting pig so that she can make a comfortable nest for her young.

rubbing with a towel, and this may prompt it to breathe.

As each piglet is born, it will be followed by its placenta, which is a jelly-like mass of tissue from which it gained nourishment as it developed. Check that each placenta is seen and removed. The exception to this one pig/one placenta rule may be in the case of twins, which can share a placenta. There are, of course, many problems that can be encountered during a birth, so it is wise to advise your vet when farrowing is due. If the female appears to be in difficulty or is obviously in a state of stress between births, consult your vet immediately. Do likewise if there is an excessive time lapse between births. This having been said, a female with a large litter may give birth to some of the babies and then take a rest before delivering the remainder. As long as she seems contented there usually is no problem. Your presence at farrowing time in order to assist and remove piglets to a warm area near the sow can make a difference in the survival rate per litter.

The stillbirth rate in pigs is about five to ten per cent. One reason for this situation can be that the temperature in the farrowing house is too low. The temperature should be no lower than 50 degrees Fahrenheit. Mummified fetuses, which are those that died in the womb after the 35th day of pregnancy, may be expelled or retained to be delivered at parturition (farrowing).

REARING PIGLETS

When they are born, the piglets are very small and may weigh as little as four ounces. It is very important that they are kept warm and that they feed as soon as possible so as to obtain colostrum from their mother's milk. This provides them with the essential antibodies needed to fight diseases. Usually, piglets will start feeding within a few minutes, though sometimes they may stand under an infrared lamp and take up to half an hour before they seek out an unoccupied nipple. A reduction in the lactation ability of the mother accounts for many piglets dying of starvation early in their life, so it is wise to have available supplementary milk. Commercial sow's milk is available for this purpose.

Handrearing or supplement feeding any juvenile animal is a time-consuming business, but it will make the difference between a young animal's surviving or dying. Feeding utensils must be scrupulously clean. As a very rough guide, if you have to handfeed a piglet, give it about 35 per cent of its daily bodyweight in milk. This should be spread over six feedings. Alternatively, use a pet's nursing bottle, and feed the piglet until it shows disinterest or dozes off to sleep. Should you suspect that a piglet is failing in health during its first few days of life, contact your vet. He may be able to tube feed the youngster in his clinic. This may be more cost effective than losing the baby.

When the little porkers are about four to five days old, they will show interest in solid foods, such as Mazuri starter 5687, which can be given to them until after they are weaned. They will need about three to four per cent of their weight per day divided into a number of meals. Although it is not the objective for your piglets to put on weight in record time, while they are babies—a critical growth period—it is better that they have adequate food rather than be short of it. This being so, let the health and vigor of the babies be your ultimate guide as to whether or not they are receiving sufficient food.

It cannot be overstressed that the care of the mother and her piglets throughout the farrowing and rearing process will prove a vital factor in determining the personality of the piglets in later life. While they must be handled on a regular basis, great care must be exercised to ensure that neither mother nor piglets are stressed from undue attention. This is especially so with regard to the mother. If she becomes frustrated by continual intrusions, this will create

Piglets should be accustomed to the presence and touch of people by the time they are weaned; but make sure you do not overdo it, thus creating stress on the mother and offspring.

A young piglet becoming acquainted with a new pal.

anxieties in the piglets. These anxieties will generalize to aggression as the youngsters get older.

SELLING THE PIGLETS

If you have correctly cared for your porcine youngsters, they will be fine healthy piglets by the time that they are ready to be sold—at about eight or more weeks of age. By this time, they should be litterbox trained and amenable to being handled. They should also have spent progressively longer periods away from their mother and siblings so that the transition from their original homes to new ones will induce the least possible trauma. You will need to make the decision as to whether or not you intend to sell the piglets as pets or as potential breeding stock. The majority of boars will be sold as pets and should be neutered. Females that are to be pets should be spayed at about six weeks of age. Unless you have extremely high-quality females and a likely market for them, it is better to regard most as being potential pets and have them spayed.

When potential purchasers contact you about the youngsters you have advertised, do try to find out if they really appreciate what owning a porky entails. In the long run, this is to every breeder's benefit. Every time a piglet goes into the wrong home, it results in negative promotion, which can only reduce future market growth. Each client should be given a diet guide and basic-care sheet. It should be stressed that if problems are encountered, you should be contacted. However, do not count on this happening. Follow up the sale with a telephone call after a few days, and then a couple of weeks later, just to see if porky has settled down well. If you are happy with the price that you obtain, you might consider giving each new owner a one-year subscription to *Pot-bellied Pigs* magazine. This little extra makes for good customer relations and may help make your customers better owners as a result of the informative articles.

Apart from consideration for your buyers, all this service makes good sales sense. The owners will be delighted with the interest that you have shown and will recommend you to other people that they meet who might also like a little porcine pal. They may also decide to purchase second piglets for themselves.

BREEDING RECORDS

Regardless of the extent of your breeding program, you will find it beneficial to maintain breeding records. Just how detailed they are will reflect both your own interest in record keeping and the kind of information that you may find useable at a later date. In general, the more detail you have, the better. Even a single-pet owner will find record keeping of benefit.

Each pig should have its own record card, and you should also have a breeding card. Each pig's card should contain such data as the sire and dam, the color and pattern, age, registration number, breeder, adult height, and weight. (Age, height, and weight should be recorded on a regular basis—from piglethood to adulthood.) Each card should also include a medical history of the pig, including vaccination records and the names of the pigs to which it has been bred. Exhibition wins can also be documented on personal records. It is very useful to attach either photos of the pig or drawings of its markings (the latter information would apply in patterned varieties). Such documentation may well be most informative in future years.

These adorable little piglets are almost ready to adopt a new family and home all their own.

When breeding potbellied pigs, make sure that you always maintain a high standard for the care, selection, and breeding process of your pigs.

The breeding card should show the names and numbers of the mated pair, when they were mated, the farrowing date, and how many piglets were born. Note colors, sexes, vaccination dates, and dates of neutering or spaying. Be very sure that you keep detailed records of their feeding regimen and, of course, all illnesses. Record the number of stillborn and the reasons (if they have been established) why they occurred. Weigh the piglets and record their gains every few days. A sudden drop in weight or the cessation of weight gain in a piglet is usually a sign of a problem. From these records you will be able to draw valuable information on the performance of sows and boars. Never rely on your memory as there is ample evidence that it is a notoriously unreliable means of documenting facts!

The foregoing should give you a good platform of information on which to build. I strongly recommend that you obtain more detailed works from your library or bookstore on commercial pig reproduction. They will detail many other aspects of the subject that are as applicable to potbellied pigs as they are to regular farm stock.

Exhibiting Pigs

To many people, the exhibition side of any pet hobby is regarded as a somewhat frivolous activity in which only a small percentage of owners involve themselves. While the second part of this comment is always a fact, the first part certainly is not. Any study of the staying power of a pet animal species will clearly show that the backbone of the hobby centers upon exhibition. It showcases a given pet, and it sets the standards by which quality is assessed.

Exhibition is the means by which breeders can come together and form clubs and associations in order to create a stable platform for their chosen pets. Consider the major pets, such as dogs, cats, horses, rabbits, cage birds, and fish and you will find that they all revolve around a very highly organized series of exhibitions. These exhibitions create a focal point for manufacturers to assess market potential for products and for the media to gain information on a particular animal. The exhibition also creates a marketplace in which buyers of pet or breeding stock from all parts of the world can go in order to see and purchase what is regarded as being the best stock available. Without the show side of the hobby, a given pet has very limited potential to become well established. Showing is thus both the window to the hobby and an ongoing program that can defend the hobby and extend its perimeters. Whether or not the show side of a hobby is actually of any specific benefit to the pet itself is a more debatable question. It is largely dependent on how concerned those who administrate the hobby are in determining what is and is not acceptable for a given pet species. For example, you do not have to look far to see the sorry state that some pets are in as a result of exhibition projection. Consider dog breeds such as the Yorkshire Terrier and the Maltese, whose mobility is restricted because of their hair length. The same is true of the Peruvian guinea pig. There are goldfish that lack dorsal fins and those with eyes situated on upward-pointing appendages. Bulldogs are testament to the fact of how far breeders will go to alter a pet's appearance. The hairless Sphinx cat survives principally because several feline associations accept it for registration and exhibition. This gives it credibility and projection. There are always those who find the bizarre both appealing and lucrative to breed.

The foregoing are examples of the adverse effects of exhibition on pet species, and they are worthy of mention because this side of the potbellied pig hobby is only just beginning. They act as an amber warning light to potbellied pig officialdom to remind them that if fashions are allowed to take precedence over the good health and well-being of potbellied pigs, the term frivolous will become justified.

It is an exciting time for potbellied pig owners and breeders. Not often in a lifetime can one be part of the initial developing history of a pet. Usually, the pet is well established, as are its breeders and top winners.

Essentially, exhibitions are a forum for breeders because these hobbyists have an ongoing situation in which fresh young

Pig-A-Dilly Kemo Sabi, pictured here with owner Mike Rich after being awarded the Altered Sex Senior Champion title in 1992 at the All American Family Pet Show in Pomona, California.

stock is always being produced. However, exhibitions are not the exclusive domain of the breeder. There are classes in which altered pigs (neutered or spayed) can compete. They enable potbellied pig owners to win exhibition honors just as is done with altered cats. It is from such exhibitors that future breeders often develop. Apart from the actual competitive side of showing, there is an equally important social aspect. At shows, you can meet other people who share your love of potbellied pigs. There are many people in the various animal hobbies that never exhibit their stock yet are avid showgoers. They enjoy the social side while also keeping abreast of what is happening in the hobby. Others breed their animals but have friends or professional handlers to take care of the exhibition side. There is thus something to interest and involve everyone in the exhibition side of a pet hobby.

THE FIRST POTBELLIED PIG SHOWS

Given the very short span of time since potbellied pigs became popular pets, they have advanced extremely rapidly in terms of associations and shows that are available for them. I am not sure of exactly when the first show was organized, but certainly one of the earliest was that called the First Annual Pet Pig Pageant. It took place in Fort Lauderdale, Florida, on October 6 and 7, 1990. It was open to any pet pig. Of the 26 entrants that came from all over the US, 25 were potbellies and one was an African Pygmy pig.

It was a very informal affair, not an organized competitive show, and it proved to be a tremendous success. The porkies and their owners stayed in the Rolling Hills Golf Resort hotel, and the entrants were walked up and down a red carpet to the delight of the well-packed audience. The media projection was fantastic, with press, radio, and national TV coverage. A number of the pigs were dressed up for the occasion, and awards were given for achievements such as "Most Fashionable," "Best Trick," "Mr. America," "Audience Choice," and "Cutest Nose." The event clearly indicated that piggy shows would be smash hits.

The next major event took place in Dallas on February 28 through March 2. It was called the First National Pig Baron's Ball, Show, and Sale, and it was another great success. Some 36 classes were scheduled, and all but five of them were serious conformation classes, such as male and female piglet, late juniors, intermediate male and female, altered sex, and get of sire. Of course there was a Best-In-Show winner, which was Fancy First Lady, an appropriate name for such a winner. In the sale, one female porky, Hi View's Rosetta, went under the hammer to a Robert Clark for the very useful price of $25,000!

With the great success of shows such as the two mentioned, it was not long before more and more shows were being staged across the US. They were sponsored by NCOPP and the North American Potbellied Pig Association (NAPPA) and judged according to the standards of these organizations. Some shows were jointly sponsored by these two groups. Thus, within two years, the exhibition side of these pets was up and running with considerable expertise being displayed. Winners such as Stormin' Norman and Winston quickly established themselves. Their offspring, along with that of the likes of Pistol Petey, are names that will be emblazoned across the pedigrees of many of the show winners of the future.

Gary Narvaez with Paradise Porkys Baily. This pig was judged Female Senior Champion and Reserve Grand Champion at the Pomona, California All American Family Pet Show in 1992.

This pig was awarded Supreme Champion Miniature Potbellied Pig in 1991 at the California State Fair and is pictured with owner Jim Carroccio of Good Day Ranch in Austin, Texas.

THE SHOW POTBELLY

One of the singular advantages of being a potential exhibitor of potbellies at this point in time is that the overall standard seen in these pets is relatively good, as compared with the situation in highly popular pets such as dogs, cats, and rabbits. This, of course, will change in the coming years; and there will be a very big difference between the best and the worst type of pigs. If you have a sound and very healthy porky, there is no reason why you should not enter it into a show and see how it fairs.

It must not be overweight, and it should not display any obvious major faults, such as cryptorchidism (lack of visible testicles in the male), hernias, or dwarfism. It will have to be registered with one of the recognized registries of the show sponsor and will have to meet the show sponsor's regulations with regard to vaccinations and any other requirements that they may apply to show stock. These requirements will include a health certificate not more than 30 days old and blood testing for pseudorabies and brucellosis.

A show potbelly should not be nervous when surrounded by strange people and other pets. It must have received basic training so that it will walk nicely on a lead, thus showing itself to its best advantage. Ring etiquette is a most important aspect of exhibiting any species.

Even if you are told that porky might never gain major honors, this does not mean that he could not pick up placings at the smaller club shows now being organized. Apart from conformation classes, you could enter him in the side or novelty classes, in

Lil Pigs Top Brass Lollipop of Divinity with owner Jane Treser after being judged as the Supreme Champion at the Los Angeles County Fair in 1992.

which conformation is not the basis of wins. Novelty classes are those such as best-dressed pig and best trick.

JUDGING

Exhibits are judged against a written standard. Each pig is assessed by the judge, and those losing the least points are the winners. Wins and placings earn points toward championship status. The points earned are dependent on how many exhibits there are in a class. Some shows may not feature point-winning classes. The regulations governing this procedure and other aspects related to exhibition vary between the show-sponsoring associations, so the potential exhibitor does need to obtain a copy of the show rules of both NAPPA and the NCOPP.

SHOW CLASSES

The following are the show-class definitions of the NCOPP:

1. Juniors: These are boars, females, and altered (neutered or spayed) juveniles that are not less than three months old and not over 12 months old on the show day.
2. Seniors: These are boars, females, and altered pigs that are over 12 months of age on the show day.
3. Get of Sire and Produce of Dam: Three individuals of at least three months of age from the same sire or dam. The three offspring are preferred to be of mixed sexes, but this is not an essential requirement.

It is required that each of the individual pigs that comprise a get of sire- or produce of dam-class must be shown in their appropriate conformation class. The exhibits may be owned by different exhibitors.

STANDARDS AND REGISTRIES

The standard used by NAPPA differs from that used by the NCOPP in terms of the points allocated. One major difference is that the NAPPA standard allocates 15 points for general appearance, which has definite benefit from a judge's viewpoint. However, in general, the application of two standards that show such a wide difference in the way points are allocated can prove to be divisive in a hobby. The existence of four or more registry associations tends to make for confusion, at least from the newcomer's viewpoint. However, this kind of situation is not uncommon as a pet makes its initial impact. It may even persist. For example, consider the seven registry associations that govern the cat-showing world in the US, each organizing its own shows and in which wins gained in one do not count in the others.

If you wish to enter shows sponsored by both of the present associations, you must have your potbelly registered with a registry that is recognized by the NCOPP and NAPPA.

HOW TO PROCEED

If the exhibition side of potbellies appeals to you, the best way to proceed is to first visit one or two shows. Talk to exhibitors and officials. Study the exhibits very closely while comparing them to the written standard. By doing so you will gain an insight into how your pig compares with different examples. If there is a potbellied pig club in your area, do join it—if not, what about starting one! Even if there are only a few owners, do bear in mind the saying "great oaks from little acorns grow."

In order to enter your pet into a show, you will have to write to the show organizer, or secretary, for a schedule and entry form. These documents will detail the classes and list the regulations with which you must comply. The larger the show the more classes there will be from which

Sir Sylvester, Altered Sex Reserve Junior Champion and Reserve Grand Champion at the 1992 All American Family Pet Show. This pig is owned by the Milligans of Lake Elsinore, California.

you can select. If you are unsure on a given point or on which classes your porky can enter, you can telephone the secretary, who will advise you based on the data that you provide.

If the show is out of state, be sure that you have the correct documentation. If porky is to be flown to the show, be sure to check with the airline as to its own regulations and requirements in terms of the travel crate. However, at first, it would make sense to wait until a show was held in your state or area so that you develop porky's show career on a step-by-step basis. See how he likes it because you want it to be a two-way deal. Some animals simply do not care for shows; others really enjoy the whole atmosphere and attention that they get.

Divinity Gardens Lil' Sugarbaby of HiView, owned by Raena Barry, placed Reserve Junior Champion at the 1991 Farmers Fair in Perris, California.

BEING A GOOD EXHIBITOR

Being that exhibition is a very young and growing part of the hobby, all exhibitors at this time have a very refreshing attitude to the sport and enter into it with enthusiasm and a strong sense of camaraderie. Do likewise and try to ensure that this always remains your objective. Unfortunately, a look at other pets will show only too well how things can change once the desire to win becomes the sole objective of participation. Exhibitors complain about each other, and, even more so, about the inadequacy of the judge. In their eyes, only they have the best exhibit, and it should win every time out!

There are those that never have time to give advice to the novice or newcomer, let alone help out a fellow exhibitor. Always try to take the bad days with the good. After all, if the same people won every time, it would soon be a pretty boring hobby and would lose its appeal. The best exhibitors learn from their failure to win, not complain about it. You enter a show to obtain the judge's opinion. Always accept it with grace. If you are convinced the judge was in error, you do not have to enter under him again. If you are right, no doubt others will take the same view; and soon the judge will get no appointments. If you are wrong, you will run out of shows to enter, which should suggest something to you!

It is true that exhibition success can bring substantial financial rewards to the top winners, especially if they are breeders. But most showgoers are never going to be flying at such dizzy heights so make the most of it by having a really good time. Remember, your mood will quickly be detected by your pets: if you are unhappy, they will soon be likewise.

THE OBEDIENCE SIDE OF THE HOBBY

At this time, the obedience side of the potbellied pig hobby is lagging behind that of the conformation side. This is to be expected because it is far more demanding of both the owner and the pig. Training classes are being organized for potbellies, and it is to be hoped that they will become an integral part of the hobby. Ultimately,

Able and willing learners, potbellies should soon gain recognition as good obedience workers.

they will result in various obedience tests being organized—rather like those offered for dogs. Indeed, I would view this development as essential: it is vital to the future of these pets that the public at large is able to see just how intelligent they are and how well they can be trained. Beauty classes can never achieve this objective.

In 1992, Karyn Garvin, a dog trainer, organized a course for porkies in Tucson, Arizona, and it was a great success. Graduation day was well attended and gained good media support. The idea of little piggies walking to heel, sitting, waiting, and standing for examination surprised many onlookers. It may be the forerunner of greater things to come. There is no doubt that pigs are extremely clever animals, and their potential in terms of obedience—and maybe even tracking—will open up a whole new side of the exhibition hobby.

In dogs, those who involve themselves in obedience work are a breed apart from those who prefer the beauty classes. If you find the training side more appealing than simply parading your pet around a show ring, why not get involved with your registration (exhibition) association and be in the vanguard of potbelly obedience stakes? Form a training club in your area. From this small beginning, we may one day see the obedience aspect of the hobby proliferate into the kind of fascinating and exciting spectacle that is seen in dogs. Bear in mind that an obedience-trained pig does not have to be a potential beauty-contest winner, and its career as a competitive pig could well be far longer than that of its beauty counterpart.

It has been many centuries since a pet came along that had the potential to rival a dog in terms of obedience classes. In the pig, such an animal exists. Obviously, it cannot do quite the same things as a dog because of conformation restrictions. But it will be exciting to see just how it develops in the coming years. All in all, the exhibition side of little porkies has to be one of the most interesting pet developments in many years, so why not get out there and be a part of it?

Health Care

Potbellied pigs are basically very healthy and strong pets provided that they are cared for correctly. If they are not, the problems and diseases that they can contract are legion—just as they are in any other animal species, including us humans. As a concerned owner, there are certain things that you can do for your pets to avoid illness or to cope with it should it happen, and there are other aspects that are not within your realm of treatment unless you happen to be a vet.

"Render unto Caesar that which is Caesar's" is a good phrase to remember with respect to the health care of your pet. By this I mean that you should draw a clear distinction between what you can do for porky and what must be left to a veterinarian. The days of home diagnosis and treatments are long since gone in an age of antibiotics, microscopy, advanced surgical techniques and their like. This acceptance of a division of skills is even more important in a pet such as a pig, which represents new ground to most owners, who are not familiar with these animals.

As a potential or existing owner, you should channel your quest for knowledge into preventive husbandry, which just happens to be the most cost-effective way of managing any pet. By adopting such a policy, the trips to your vet will hopefully be minimal. When such a journey is necessary, your general common-sense approach and observations will be such that you can give your vet considerable help. Supply a sound case history of your pet, and carefully detail the problem with which you are confronted.

RECOGNIZING UNHEALTHY STOCK

If you have gone about the process of seeking out a reputable breeder when obtaining your piglet, there will be little risk that you will have been sold anything other than a healthy youngster. Even so, you should know how to spot an unhealthy piglet. Otherwise, how will you know when your piggie is ill? In assessing poor health, the first indication of it is often seen in behavioral changes, so always be aware of what is normal for each pet that you own. Any deviation from what you normally observe will be for a reason.

Some examples of behavioral changes are: a very greedy eater that suddenly shows disinterest in its favorite food items, is much less active than normal, or is sleeping rather longer than usual. Or, maybe porky hasn't slopped his water all over the kitchen or shows no interest in clambering all over you. Each of these behavioral changes will usually derive from an internal disturbance that has not yet developed sufficiently to display clinical signs. Such a problem may be only of a temporary nature. Perhaps it is the result of earlier overeating that has created an upset stomach, or because the pet was exercised more than normal so it is more sleepy. But you will not know immediately whether or not such a change is temporary or the first sign of a more serious condition. Behavioral changes are thus a warning that you should observe your porky more carefully over the next 24 hours, by which time temporary conditions should correct themselves.

Do not ignore your "hunches." Sometimes your pet's behavior is not all that different yet you just have a

Learn to recognize when your pig is not feeling well. It will help you to detect an illness at an early stage. Signs of an unwell pet may be lack of appetite, lack of energy, or moodiness. This pig looks healthy.

feeling that something is not as it should be. When you get this kind of feeling, it is a good sign in one sense because it means you have obviously studied your pet very well and know his every mood. Most often all is well, but "feelings" alert you to be extra watchful, and this makes for good management.

Other than changes in behavior, the most obvious signs of ill health will be physical. As a general rule, the greater the number of clinical signs and behavioral changes that are evident, the more serious is the condition. But some diseases may show no outward signs, and the only indication you may get is that your little friend will become listless and go off its food. The first rule is, therefore, that if your pet's behavioral changes do not improve within 36 hours at the most, call your vet. The sooner the vet can commence a diagnosis via tests, the greater the chances of a quick recovery at the least cost to you and less distress to porky.

With respect to clinical signs, each of the following suggests a problem of greater or lesser seriousness:

1. Running eyes or nose. The cause may be an external irritant or it may be an internal problem related to the eyes or nose.

2. Excessive snorting or any wheezy breathing. This would suggest a respiratory problem.

3. Diarrhea. (This is mainly the result of other physical problems rather than being a condition in and of itself). Loose bowels can be the result of a chill, overeating, or the pig's eating something that did not agree with it. Each of these conditions are relatively minor, but virtually every killer disease will also be accompanied by loose bowels.

4. Repeated vomiting. Most animals will vomit at some time or

another; but when it is repeatedly, something is amiss.

5. Swellings, sores, or abrasions. In and of themselves, these conditions may only be minor problems. However, if untreated, they may prove to be the site of secondary infections, which could be extremely serious. The pig will either attempt to scratch itself or will be constantly rubbing against a hard object. This action is not to be confused with your pet just having a periodic scratch or rub, which is characteristic of most mammals from time to time.

6. Blood-streaked fecal matter. Clearly this is a serious condition.

7. Lameness. This may be the result of a minor strain, a broken limb, a damaged hoof, a dietary deficiency, a disease, or it could be a genetic problem that cannot be cured.

8. Fits or convulsions. These problems could be the result of poison, shock, or could be a genetic nervous disorder.

9. Emaciation. A pig may lose weight without displaying other clinical signs of ill health.

10. Reproductive Failure. Any drop in the number of piglets in a litter from that which was considered normal or a high incidence of mummified fetuses would suggest that the female is infected with any of a number of pathogens (disease-causing organisms) that invade the reproductive tract.

Young piglets need to be kept warm. Continual chills and drafts will lower its ability to ward off pathogens.

GENERAL MANAGEMENT

While it would seem superfluous to discuss aspects of general management beyond that already dealt with, the fact is that it is from a breakdown in general management that the vast majority of problems and diseases arise. Disease may reach your piglet via many routes, which include the following: direct or proximinal contact with other pigs (including boars used on your females), airborne transmission, via animals other than pigs (including insects and other invertebrates), on the clothing of humans, via its food, via feeding utensils, via its exercise areas (such as pasture), and via rotting vegetation or piles of fecal matter.

Bear in mind also that many pathogens are actually living continually within the body of your pet and are held in check by the good health of porky. This being the case, they can never reproduce to the degree that they are able to overwhelm the natural immune system. If you understand the ways in which pathogens are transmitted, you can concentrate your efforts into at least minimizing the risk that they will invade your pet. Clearly, a breeder's stock is at greater risk to pathogenic attack than is the single pet because of the greater number of pigs being housed.

The first line of defense against illness must come from good nutrition. It gives porky the needed vitamins and minerals to ensure that his body has the required ammunition to wage war on pathogens—should they arrive. Next, hygiene levels must be of the highest

Through good hygiene practices and nutrition, throughout a pig's life, one can reduce the chance of piggy catching any serious illness. This also holds true for other pets as well.

order. Food and water dishes should be washed daily. Any that get chipped or cracked should be replaced. Bedding should be cleaned on a very regular basis, and outdoor accommodations should be hosed at least once a week.

All used bedding material, such as hay, straw, or wood shavings, should not be left near the housing but should be removed and thrown away. Likewise, fecal matter, which might be used as manure, should also be kept well away from the housing. All food items should be stored in a cool dry cupboard and ideally kept in airtight containers. Always wash your hands after attending to routine chores. Disposable surgical gloves are useful if you have to handle an ill pig.

If outdoor housing is used, it is best to purchase rubber boots in order to attend to chores. They can be cleaned with a suitable disinfectant. You should be diplomatic if pig-owning friends visit you and you know they have recently had an illness problem with their pigs. Two factors that are critically important with pigs are temperature and stress control. Above 80 degrees Fahrenheit, two things can happen. First, your pet will become too hot, and this will create severe stress (a condition in itself). In turn, resistance to disease will be lowered. Second, the heat will increase the reproductive capacity of pathogens, so that you are faced with a two-sided situation. With respect to lower temperatures, you can work on the basis that if you feel cold (which usually is the case when the temperature is below 50 degrees Fahrenheit), your pet pig will feel even colder. Thus, stress will be induced and food-energy loss will increase as the pig's body combats the cold.

STRESS

It is now generally agreed that stress may well be one of the most important reasons not only for raising the likelihood of an illness but also for creating abnormal behavioral changes. The problem with stress is that you cannot see it or touch it, so it is very difficult to pinpoint its cause. Furthermore, what might create stress in one individual may not do so in another. This having been said, there are certain conditions that will definitely induce stress. The only variable will be the consequences of it.

One of the most important aspects of good management for a single pet, breeding stock, or an entire menagerie is – a vet.

Overcrowding, lack of bedding, malnutrition, bullying, lack of exercise, boredom, fright, excessive disturbance, unwanted petting, confinement, and transportation are all classic examples of stress inducers. They are all general conditions that would apply to any animal (including humans). In the case of pigs, the lack of a rooting facility and inadequate chewing potential (no provision of hay or similar foraging food) in the diet can be added to this list.

The effects of stress, apart from dramatically lowering resistance to illness, may include any of the following: aggressive behavior such as biting or charging, pacing, excessive drinking (if water is ad lib), coprophagy (eating fecal matter), urine-drinking, tail-biting, bar-biting (on the metal of their stall), prolonged sucking, body-biting, vacuous chewing (on nothing), snout- or head-rubbing, cannibalism and other maternal failures, functional inertia (refusal to move in spite of strong persuasion), and acute nervousness. The list could go on, but the foregoing should serve to illustrate just how dramatic an effect stress can have.

Eliminating the causes will often relieve the stress but not always the consequence of it. This will depend on the degree to which the behavior pattern is imprinted in the individual.

It is important that you understand the significance of general husbandry techniques in maintaining your pet in a healthy condition and why practical preventive knowledge is so much more important to the pet owner and breeder than reading volumes about specific diseases and their treatments. Most of these subjects would be far too technical for the average person to absorb or to apply, even if they understood a good part of the matter.

GENERAL CARE

So far in this discussion of health, the text has been devoted to what might be regarded as environmental aspects. We can now turn our attention to a hands-on approach with respect to general care and minor

It can be easy to miss problems that might occur with a potbelly if managing more than a few; that's why it is important to check your pigs frequently for any problems, such as with its skin, hooves, and ears to name a few.

treatments. You should regularly check your piggie. Ensure that you keep him clean, and check his body for any signs of problems. A good hand-held magnifying glass is a useful item to have when inspecting specific areas of the skin.

Ears: Ears should be inspected and wiped clean on a weekly basis. A weak solution of glycerine and warm water can be used to wipe the inner-ear flap using cotton swabs. You can also gently wipe inside the ear, but never probe too far as doing so might create problems. A foul discharge from the ear or the presence of heavy waxing is best referred to your vet. Any lesions on the ears should be wiped with warm water and a suitable antiseptic applied to them. Any scaly or encrusted areas suggest parasitic infestation and will require veterinary inspection in order to establish their cause. This is rather important because certain skin problems, such as sarcoptic mange, are zoonotic (transmissible to humans). Ear wounds resulting from fighting are a potential cause of swine necrosis, which can be quite serious if not treated promptly.

Skin Parasites: The folds of skin found on the head (snout and around the eyes) and on the tail root are an obvious haven for numerous parasites. Check the folds weekly, and wipe them with a saline solution. In the event that any parasites (mites, ticks, and the like) are seen on your pet, they can be readily eradicated using a suitable insecticidal treatment from your vet. It is better that this type of medication is obtained from a vet because it will be a target compound, which will be more effective than a general treatment—assuming that your vet has identified the parasite. There are

To ensure that her piggy will never suffer from discomfort due to hoof problems, this pig owner will need to maintain the hooves through proper trimming and conditioning throughout the life of her pet.

a considerable number of external parasites, including flies, mosquitoes, and their like, that feed briefly on your pig, as opposed to those such as lice and mites, which live and breed on the host. Those that remain on your pet's body can be a constant problem and health threat. Apart from treating your pet, it is important that the bedding material is treated as well (if it is a fabric material) in order to eradicate the larvae as they hatch from eggs laid in the material. In bad cases of infestation, the bedding material should be discarded; and carpets, furniture, etc., used by the pig should be treated.

Teeth: Although much easier said than done, you should endeavor to inspect and clean your pet's teeth. You can use a regular toothbrush or rub the teeth with a cloth wetted with a saline solution. The tusks should be trimmed as needed, which can mean every six months to every two years, according to the sex and individual. Your vet can attend to this for you as tranquilizers will be required. If the protruding tusks are not trimmed, they can cause serious injury to you or others. This is especially true of a boar, whose tusks are large. Such injury may be accidental, but the resulting wounds and pain do not differentiate between accidents and deliberate malice!

Hooves: Your pet's hooves should be routinely inspected to see that they are not in any way damaged. Check the sole to see that it is free of small objects that might impede comfort when your pig is walking. On average, the hooves will need trimming once a year. You can help keep the hooves at a sound length by using a file.

I would suggest that you do a little research into the anatomy of the two main digits (third and fourth medials) because it is important that you know what you are doing if you attempt to trim the hooves. The two small digits (second and fifth laterals) are more easily dealt with as they do not touch the floor and are very much smaller (the first digit is no longer present in pigs).

The bulk of your pet's weight is taken by the rear half of the abaxial (outer) wall and heel. The abaxial wall grows faster than does the axial (inner) part of the wall. When the hoof is trimmed, it is thus a matter of some importance that it is done in such a way that the weight remains dispersed in the manner just stated. If not, lameness may develop. Trimming can be done with horse hoof nippers or a Swiss hoof knife. Even an electric sander can be used, although this would likely frighten a small pet such as a potbelly.

The best time to effect annual trimming is in the winter months, when the growth rate is somewhat slower. Not all vets are able to provide a good trimming service, so try to locate one (maybe one who attends cattle) who is skilled at this important task. It is sometimes incorrectly stated that trimming a pig's hooves is rather like trimming a dog's claws. This is not so because a dog does not walk on its nails as does a pig. Trimming angulations are important to a pig. There are several products available that can be used to keep your pig's hooves in good condition.

Skin: The skin of a young piglet is very soft and supple, but it gets harder as the animal ages. The hair is, of course, minimal on a pig and varies in length on an individual basis. If your pet is fed a correct diet, the skin will be in healthy condition. Some owners apply one of the numerous skin conditioners now marketed for these pets, but they are not essential. You can apply a solution of glycerin and water if you wish; but bear in mind that if the pig has access to an outdoor paddock, any lotions on the skin will attract dirt.

Basically, the pig's skin was never intended to be moist other than when the pig periodically wallows in water to cool itself. Additionally, the pig was not evolved to live in a centrally heated home. There is, therefore, merit in giving porky a mist spray each week to provide the skin with moisture. If he gets dirty, you can by all means bathe him. Be sure the water is neither hot nor cold. Do not allow water to enter the ears or eyes. A mild shampoo is the favored choice, but ensure that porky is well rinsed so that there is no residual shampoo left on the the skin. This can cause an irritation. Needless to say, your pet should not be allowed out on bath day if the weather is cold.

VACCINATIONS

Not only are vaccinations your best means of protecting your pet from major diseases but also some of them will be obligatory if you keep a pet. If you plan to breed your pets, then more vaccinations will be required. Exactly how many are appropriate for potbellies is somewhat of a bone of contention. The house pet is not at the same risk to porcine diseases as are pigs kept in a commercial setting. Furthermore, excessive numbers of vaccinations can induce stress and not all of them have a proven record of efficacy. Generally, there is no benefit in vaccinating for all diseases simply because a vaccine exists. Vaccinations should be especially appropriate to an owner's situation.

Following is a listing of a number of the major diseases against which you can gain protection for your pet. Your pet's vaccination program should reflect your pet's needs (based on your locality) and the recommendations of your veterinarian. Always bear in mind that no vaccine is 100 per cent effective because of the varying virulence of different strains of a pathogen. Furthermore, the

Since a pig's tusks can cause injury, it is a good idea to have them regularly trimmed.

health of your pig at the time of vaccination can also affect the efficacy of a given vaccine.

Swine erysipilas: This is a highly contagious disease that causes septicemia (blood disease), arthritis, lesions, and other problems. The causal agent, *Erysipelothrix rhusiopathiae*, is able to live in soil, water, and rotting organic matter. Pigs that have recovered from this disease may be carriers for life. This disease is resistant to most commonly used disinfectants (phenol, hydrogen peroxide, formaldehyde) but is destroyed by caustic soda and hypochlorites. Vaccinate at four to six weeks of age with a repeat three weeks later, and thereafter biannually.

Leptospirosis: This contagious disease causes fever, anorexia, hemorrhage, circling, intestinal problems, and reproductive failure or reduced performance. The causal pathogenic group (*Leptospira* spp) is often found in water contaminated by the urine of the pig and other domestic or wild carriers. Food may also be contaminated by the pig and, for example, by rodents. A treated pig may continue to pass the pathogens in its urine for up to 12 months. Vaccination is mandatory as this disease is zoonotic. Vaccinate at four to six weeks of age with a repeat three weeks later, and thereafter biannually.

Through regular cleaning and disinfecting, harmful germs and bacteria can be reduced or eliminated from a pig's environment.

Atrophic rhinitis: This respiratory disease causes sneezing, runny eyes, and abnormal development of the jaws and snout. The etiology suggests that at least two organisms are involved. *Bordetella* sp and *Pasteurella* spp are the most widely suggested. Young pigs are prone to this disease at three to eight weeks of age. The severity of this condition is linked to the degree of immunity that was received from the sow. The porcine exhibitor's stock or agricultural showgoer's stock is more at risk to this disease than is that of the stay-at-home owner. Vaccination is generally recommended, but its efficacy is debatable according to some authorities on immunology. Vaccinations are given at any time after one week of age according to the vet's recommendations. Good hygiene and ample ventilation in housing are the suggested preventatives, but they would normally only be applicable to breeders with herds in outdoor accommodations.

There are a number of other respiratory conditions and diseases in pigs. They include mycoplasmal pneumonia, necrotic rhinitis, pasteurellosis, pleuropneumonia, and swine influenza. All of them may show some similarity in clinical signs so qualified diagnosis is required. Treatments vary as does the recovery expectancy for them.

Gastrointestinal diseases: Under this heading come a number of diseases that manifest themselves in diarrhea. Included among them are transmissible gastroenteritis (TGE), rotavirus, coronavirus, *Escherichia coli*, *Clostridium* type C, salmonellosis, *Eimeria*, and *Candida*. They are caused by viruses, bacteria, protozo-

Just like many other domestic animals, pigs need to be vaccinated against certain contagious and harmful diseases.

ans and fungi. They are all contagious. In some instances (e.g., TGE), vaccines are available; some are more effective than others. Prebreeding vaccination is recommended, but the thrust of management should always be directed at prevention by hygiene and similar husbandry techniques already discussed.

Porcine parvovirus: This is a disease of the reproductive tract and results in mummified fetuses and general reproductive failure. Vaccination of breeding sows is obligatory and is effected twice prior to breeding, thereafter biannually.

Pseudorabies (Aujeszky's disease or mad itch): The effects of this viral disease of the central nervous system are sneezing and coughing followed by anorexia. Trembling, lack of coordination, and coma may also be evident. The pig is the only known reservoir of this disease, which can be transmitted to other animals. It can be fatal in young pigs but rarely so in adults, though they will act as carriers. All breeding stock should be tested quarterly for this disease, which has many strains. Stock purchased for breeding should be tested seronegative before being introduced to other stock. Vaccines are available for prevention, but there is no control treatment at this time. Other pets infected by pigs will normally die, but humans are resistant to the disease. States differ in their regulations regarding this disease, so check with your vet and/or the Department of Agriculture. Infected pigs may have to be slaughtered; so if a herd situation exists, it is wise to deny the public access to the herd because of the risk that it may introduce the pathogens. If you exhibit your pigs, be especially careful to avoid—where possible—places where farmyard pigs are present. Some states prohibit vaccination because this makes blood testing inconclusive.

Tetanus: This condition is brought about by anaerobic (non-oxygen breathing) organisms (*Clostridium* spp) that live in the soil. They produce neurotoxins that affect the nervous system, resulting in muscle spasms to any part of the body. In pigs, arching of the back and neck (opisthotonos) is often displayed when the animal is startled. It may also fall to the ground. The anaerobes access the body via wounds and similar lesions. Keep wounds and lesions clean, including those created as a result of desexing in young piglets. A vaccine is available.

Rabies: This is a dreaded disease of the nervous system. It is not common in pigs, but all mammals are at risk that do not live in "rabies-free" areas (Great Britain, Australia, and Hawaii are among the few "rabies-free" areas of the world). There is no vaccine available specifically for pigs, but those for other pets are sometimes used (in special quantity) in high-risk areas.

ENTROPION AND THE EYES

This condition is evidenced by an inverted eyelid that results in one or more eyelashes rubbing against the cornea and conjunctiva. The result is varying degrees of discomfort and irritation. The condition is genetic; so when it is confirmed, the affected pig should not be used for breeding. The condition can be rectified by surgical removal of some of the skin of the eyelid. If no action is taken, not only will the pig suffer greatly but also more permanent eye damage may result.

Not all instances of apparent entropion are the "real thing." There are numerous other ways in which a look-alike condition can result in similar clinical signs. For example, a slightly swollen eyelid, a misdirected cilia, a foreign body in the eye, or even sunburn, will create a change in the eyelid that might direct the lashes onto the eye. Potbellied pigs also have varying degrees of skin wrinkles around the eye, and these too can cause similar problems. If your pet displays signs of eye irritation, do not simply apply eye lotions. Let your vet examine porky so a correct diagnosis can be made.

INTERNAL PARASITES

In general, this term relates to worms of various species. All pets will have worms in their bodies. These parasites (e.g., roundworms and tapeworms) become a problem when their level of infestation is such that it adversely affects metabolic processes to the degree that illness results. High worm-levels debilitate the host, which reduces the pig's ability to resist other parasites. In severe cases, the pig may lose weight

If a pig is to live entirely outside, make sure it has adequate shelter so that it may retreat from the sun and other undesirable weather conditions. In the summer, a wading pool is recommended.

as well as its normal interest in its food. Your vet can do worm counts from fecal examinations. Piglets should be routinely wormed at about four weeks of age and a repeat dose given three weeks later. Adults can, of course, be treated at any time. Once worm infestation has been confirmed, hygiene is essential as the unhatched eggs of the parasites will be present wherever the pig has defecated. The likelihood of worms in the average potbelly is low if hygiene is of a good standard and the pig is not exposed to other pigs or livestock.

HYPERTHERMIA (SUNBURN AND HEATSTROKE)

With very little hair to safeguard it, the pig is easily affected by the intense rays of the sun. White pigs are especially prone to sunburn. Always ensure that there is some shady spot for your pet if it is in an outside enclosure. Sunscreens with a sun protection factor of 15 or over will effectively block sun rays, but the use of them should be restricted to occasions when, for whatever reason, shade is not available. When traveling in a vehicle, it is crucial that porky never gets too hot. *Never* leave your pet in a vehicle on a hot day with the windows completely closed. In the event that your pet displays signs of heatstroke, such as vomiting, collapsing, or glassy eyes, it is crucial that your response is immediate. Immerse the pig in cool water or use water-soaked towels in order to help bring his temperature down rapidly. Once the pig appears to be breathing and acting normally, it would be wise to let a veterinarian check him over because a side effect might be shock.

ZOONOSES

Zoonoses are diseases that can be transferred from your pig (and other pets) to you. The chance of their occurring is low, assuming that you are careful about personal hygiene. Those who keep a herd should be especially aware of the need to maintain high personal-hygiene standards at all times and particularly if any of the stock has contracted a zoonotic disease. The following is but a short listing of some zoonoses of pigs:

Although there are some diseases that can be transmitted from pigs to people, it is highly unlikely unless one has poor hygiene habits.

Anthrax: This is a bacterial killer-disease that strikes warm-blooded animals. It is worldwide in distribution and can especially be a problem in areas such as the southern US.

Brucellosis: A bacterial disease transmitted by direct contact with secretions, including milk, of infected animals.

Chagas disease: Protozoan infection of bite wounds.

Clostridial diseases (including tetanus): A bacterial disease usually transmitted via soil spores that make contact with a wound. It can also be contracted from an infected animal.

Erysipelas: Bacterial disease contracted from infected animal via wounds or other body lesions.

Leptospirosis: Bacterial disease transmitted by direct contact with an infected animal's urine.

Melioidosis: Bacterial disease contracted via soil or water contamination of lesions or by inhalation.

Porcine Tapeworm: Ingestion of eggs via contaminated and undercooked pork foods.

Ringworm: Fungal infection contracted by direct contact with an infected animal.

Salmonellosis: Bacterial disease contracted by the direct handling of and more often by the ingestion of undercooked infected foods.

Trichinosis (roundworm): Ingestion of undercooked infected pork-foods.

INJURIES AND SHOCK

Should your pet be injured, no matter what the cause, the first thing to do is to try and keep it calm. Minor cuts will not, of course, bother the pet but should be cleaned and then treated with an antiseptic or a coagulant such as a styptic pencil. More serious cuts will need cleaning and then covering with a suitable material while the pig is transported to the vet for proper care. In the event of a broken limb, try to restrain the pet before traveling to your vet. Depending on your pet's size, you might be able to wrap him in a blanket.

In the event of shock, such as after being bitten or badly frightened by a dog, calm the pet and place him in a darkened room. If the pig has collapsed, carefully move him to a quiet spot and cover him with a blanket. However, do not create too much heat—keep porky just comfortably warm. In all cases of accidents, what is important is that you do not get hysterical as this will merely transfer to your pig, who will become even more frightened.

IDENTIFICATION

In order for a pig to be registered with one of the potbelly pig associa-

Regularly spending time with your pig on a one-to-one basis will strengthen the pet/owner relationship and foster your pig's sense of well-being.

tions, it must have some form of permanent identification mark. Such identification will also be required if pigs are sold interstate. The options are: metal or plastic ear tags, ear notches, tattoos (on the ear flap or flank), and microchip implants. A tattoo on the inner ear flap or an implant are perhaps the most acceptable choices for the pet owner as either one is less obvious and unsightly compared to tags.

The procedure for tattooing is straightforward and can be performed on a young piglet by a veterinarian. Choose an ink color appropriate to the ear color so that it is legible without being too obvious. The letter/number size should be about three/eighths of an inch. The NCOPP includes a microchip with its registration and can even arrange for you to obtain a tool so that you can do the tattooing yourself (or it can be done by your vet). The microchip is likely to be the most-used form of identification in future years because of its flexibility in the way it can store information.

QUARANTINE

Given the very strict regulations that apply to all farm livestock, any potbellied pig owner who plans to have or has a breeding program is strongly advised to have some means of isolating any of his pigs. This is most important where the acquisition of additional stock is concerned. It is also a very wise practice—but often ignored—where exhibition stock is concerned. The minimum period of quarantine should be 14 days, although 21 would be better.

During the isolation period, new stock, or that having returned from exhibitions, can be carefully monitored. When the isolation period is over, the pig can be returned to its normal quarters. In the case of breeding stock, especially newly acquired animals, do not immediately place them into a herd situation after the quarantine period. Instead, put them into a pen within the housing facility. This practice allows them to be exposed to any localized bacteria without direct contact with the resident stock. This, of course, works both ways and exposes the residents to any bacteria carried by the newcomer. The greater the number of pigs you own the more important it is that you quarantine all incoming stock.

Remember, you are as responsible for protecting your area from the spread of disease as is the largest cattle or swine rancher—or other farm-livestock breeder. Avoid mixing species if you have a herd situation.

This pig has an ear tag for identification; but tattooing and microchips are also available.

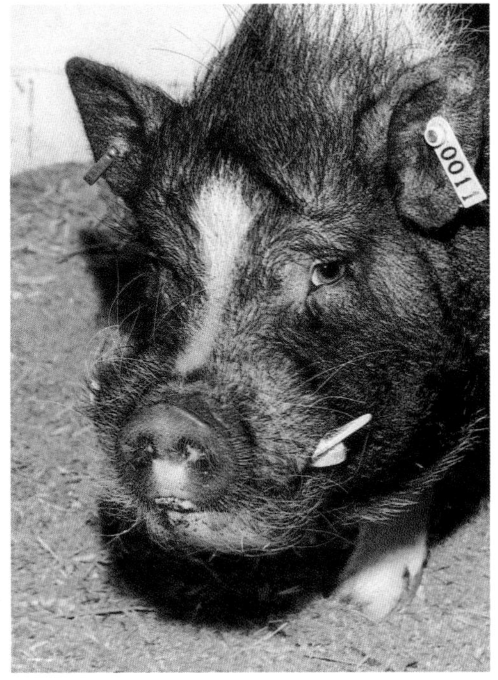

Natural History

In this chapter, we will view the potbellied pig from a purely zoological standpoint. Many people that are involved in a given hobby know little about the natural history of the species that they keep. The following text will help round out your knowledge of your porcine pet and will serve as a point of reference to what certain terms mean should you come across them in other texts.

SCIENTIFIC CLASSIFICATION

By understanding natural classification, you will learn much about the anatomy and ethology of your pet. The wild ancestor of the potbellied pig is called *Sus scrofa*—the wild boar or pig. No other organism on this planet has this name, and it is international in use. If a person from China, France, or Russia understands zoological nomenclature and you say *Sus scrofa* to him, he will know exactly which species you are referring to if he has any interest in pigs. The use of such terminology thus represents one of the truly great examples of how we humans can get together and agree to apply a single policy on a global basis.

A SYSTEM OF RANKS OR GROUPS

So that zoologists (and any interested person) can talk to each other and refer to either specific animals or groups of similar kinds of animals, a system was evolved during the 18th century for just this purpose. The founder of scientific nomenclature, taxonomy, or animal systematics (whichever term is preferred) was a Swedish naturalist named Carolus Linnaeus.

It utilizes Latin as the basis of the system. While this might seem a strange choice, there were good reasons for so doing. Firstly, it was the language of scholars, and secondly, being a "dead" language, it was more readily acceptable to scientists of all nations. The system is called the binomial system of nomenclature. To appreciate how it works, you might consider a triangle. The apex is life itself. In other words, the system embraces all of the animals in the world—from those that are microscopic to those such as the blue whale, the largest living creature. They form the kingdom known as Animalia. The kingdom is divided into a number of groups, and in each group the animals share certain features. Such features are very basic near the top of the system but become more and more complex as you move downward toward the base, which contains each animal species.

For example, there is a rank called a class. In it, the various animals display given features. There are classes called Mammalia, Insecta, Aves (birds), Reptilia, Osteicthyes (bony fish), and many others. In some classes, such as Aves, a single diagnostic feature may be displayed by the members (in this case feathers), but in most, it is by consideration of many features that a given animal will be placed in a particular group. A pig is a mammal, which means it is warm-blooded (homoiothermic), has hair, develops its young in a placenta, suckles its young, and breathes air via lungs. We are mammals, as are lions, dogs, sheep, and even whales and dolphins, which might surprise some readers. All mammals are thus more closely related to each other than they are to members of another class. They have a common phylogenic history.

Each class is divided into ranks

called orders, of which there are many in each class. Within Mammalia there are, among others, Rodentia (rodents), Primates (man and monkeys), Carnivora (flesh eaters such as dogs, cats, bears, and others), Lagomorpha (rabbits, hares, and pikas), Perissodactyla (horses, tapirs, zebras, rhinos) and Artiodactyla. The pig is in the last group. Again, all the members of each order share many features, some of which are not always apparent based purely on external appearance.

The orders are divided into families, and pigs are in the family called Suidae. Families are divided into genera (singular, genus) and porky is in that known as *Sus*. By now we are getting very close to our target pet. The genera are divided into species, within which the specimens are looking very similar indeed. Even so, in some instances, differences in local populations can be observed so an additional rank called the subspecies is recognized.

The species is designated by adding a trivial or specific name to the name of the genus, thus forming a binomial, the basis of the system. For the wild boar the trivial name is *scrofa*. Thus, the name *Sus scrofa* distinguishes this species from *Sus salvanius*, the pygmy hog, or from *Sus verrucosus*, the Javan or warty pig. The generic, species, and subspecies names are conventionally written in a type that is different from the main text, which is why you will see them printed in italics. The generic name always starts with a capital letter, while the specific name always commences with a lower-case letter.

It is important to note that only when the binomial is used can a species be identified. Thus, *scrofa* does not designate the pig because it could be used in another animal group; but when combined with *Sus*, it creates uniqueness. The system does not make special provision for

A pig's canine teeth, as well as the deciduous teeth, begin erupting prior to birth.

domesticated variants derived from a natural species, so all miniature domesticated pigs are simply *Sus scrofa*, and designation of a particular variety would be made clear within the text of a given language.

LOOKING AT THE PORCINE RANKS

Having given an overview of the way zoological nomenclature works, let us now look more closely at the groups discussed that are applicable to pigs. Artiodactyla: This order comprises the even-toed ungulates—as compared to the order Perissodactyla, which are the odd-toed ungulates. The word *ungulate* means hoofed: A hoof is actually the equivalent of our nails but very much stronger. Pigs and many other ungulates have cloven hooves, which means that the hoof is divided, or cleft. There are some 9 families, 81 genera, and 211 species within the order Artiodactyla. They include pigs, peccaries, hippos, llamas, camels, deer, giraffes, and all of the bovids, such as goats, sheep, cattle, and antelopes. They are worldwide in distribution but not indigenous to Australia, New Zealand, Antarctica, the West Indies, New Guinea, and many oceanic islands. (Many ungulates have been introduced to these areas by humans.)

Within the order, some members are

ruminants, meaning that they can chew their cud (regurgitated food passed through a three- or four-chambered stomach). Pigs and other suids have only a two-chambered stomach so they do not practice this method of food digestion. Most members of the order are herbivorous in their diet, but some, e.g., pigs and peccaries, are omnivorous. While there are many features that make an animal an artiodactyl, you will note that the possession of a hoof is a most important characteristic.

Suidae: This family contains five genera and nine species. Apart from having the features of the order, they are differentiated from other families by the following: They are medium-sized, stocky animals with a body length reaching about 190cm (75 in.) and a tail of some 45cm (18 in). The head is elongated and ends with a truncated snout. The snout has a disk-like end, which is cartilaginous and is used for rooting. The skin is thick, dry, and sparsely coated with hair, which is almost absent in some genera.

The young of all genera, with the exception of *Babyrousa* and domestic forms of *Sus scrofa*, are striped. The ears are erect and often feature small tassels of hair at their tips. The tail is straight except in many domestic forms of *Sus scrofa* and is often tufted with hair at its tip. Facial warts are a feature of some members of the family. There are four toes on each foot. The third and fourth medials are larger and are used to bear the weight of the animal. The shorter second and fifth digits do not touch the floor and are located on the rear of each foot. The first digit is no longer present.

The number of teeth is 34 or 44, according to genera. The canine teeth are long, sharp, and curve upward and backwards. They are present in both sexes but are larger in the male. The teeth tend to completely wear away with age, the exceptions being the molars and the canines. There are a number of other anatomical features of the family, but they need not be discussed here.

Pigs live in wooded habitats and are mainly nocturnal, feeding on roots, bulbs, fruit, grain, worms, eggs, small reptiles, carrion, and most anything else that comes their way. They are timid creatures but courageous fighters when attacked. For shelter, they will use tall grass, the burrows of other animals, or self-made burrows. The females have three or six pairs of mammae in most genera (*Babyrousa* has only one pair). All pigs are surprisingly sure-footed and capable of speed when it is warranted—flight being their first line of defense. Pigs are excellent swimmers, and their famed love of mud baths is typical of the family. Distribution is throughout Eurasia, Africa, and as far as Sulawesi and the Philippines.

Sus: There are five species within this genus, which was named by Linnaeus in 1758. Shoulder height may range to 110cm (43 in.), and body weight may reach 350kg (770 lb). This weight may be exceeded by up to 40 per cent in some domestic variants of *Sus scrofa*. In comparison to the large species of the genus, the pygmy hog, *S. salvanius*, attains a shoulder height of only 30cm (12 in.).

Sus scrofa: This species is commonly known as the wild boar, or pig. The color is gray-brown to black. A mane is often present, especially in males, which are normally larger than females.

A herd, or sounder, typically consists of up to 20 individuals of varying ages, but it may reach 100 in isolated areas where interference by humans is minimal. The social life of pigs revolves around small family units consisting of a sow and her offspring.

The females leave family units in order to mate with the otherwise solitary adult boars. The gestation period is 100-140 days; the estrus cycle is usually 21 days, with the heat lasting for two to three days. Interestingly, the young are not normally weaned until they are three to four months of age, and young females will often remain with the sow until she is due to give birth to another litter. Unlike most other ungulates, the babies will remain in their nest for a greater length of time (two to three days) than is typical for this group of animals.

Although sexual maturity in the female is reached as early as eight months of age, she will probably not mate until she is about 18 months old, by which time she is physically mature. A boar, in comparison, may not be able to mate until he is approaching five years of age. This is due to the fact that until then, he is not strong enough to assert himself when competing with established males that are more powerful.

When fighting, wild pigs will normally shoulder-shove each other at first and then rear up in an effort to knock their opponents off their feet. If this fails to establish psychological superiority, they will turn and face each other in serious combat. Their power and razor-sharp tusks can inflict terrible wounds on each other before one of them decides to call it a day. A wild boar is not the kind of critter that you would want to meet on a stroll through a forest! Potentially more dangerous than pigs are the peccaries (javelinas), which are in a related family and are the New World equivalent to the Old World pigs. They will invariably attack as a group and seem to get more furious when one of their kind is injured or killed.

DOMESTICATION

The domestication of *Sus scrofa* is thought to have taken place in China about 4,900 B.C., but experts think it could have been very much earlier, circa 10,000 B.C. The latter date would make the pig second only to the dog in terms of domestic history. The pig is thought to have arrived in the US via both Hawaii (Polynesian travelers) and South America (Spaniards). Further infusions followed from Europe in order to establish the species for hunting purposes. Many of these wild boars subsequently mated with domestic pigs, and some of the offspring became feral. There are now large populations of these feral pigs in certain states of the US, as well as in many other countries of the world.

There really are not that many species of wild pig left on our planet so it is to be hoped that the popularity of the potbelly may prove of benefit in making people aware of the plight of some of these species. In enjoying your little pet pig, give a thought to its wild brethren that are struggling just to survive. Give your support to the conservation of the forests of the world; it will be a major step forward in helping the plight of these wild pigs.

A couple physiological facts about potbellied pigs: the heart rate is 55 to 86 beats per minute (depending on the level of physical activity or stress), and the respiratory rate is 20 to 30 breaths per minute.

Glossary

Abaxial—The outer wall of a cloven hoof
Axial—The inner wall of a cloven hoof
Barrow—A neutered male
Boar—An intact or unaltered male
Bred Gilt—A female that is pregnant with her first litter
Cloven hoof—A hoof in which the two large digits are split
Farrow—The process of giving birth to piglets
Feeders—A young weaned pig that is feeding independently
Gilt—A female pig that has never farrowed
Hog—A swine of 120 lbs. (54.5kg) or heavier
Neuter—To render a boar incapable of reproduction
Pig—A swine under 120 lbs. (54.5kg)
Piglet—A baby pig
Sow—A female pig that has been bred from or that is one or more years of age
Sounder—An alternative term for a herd of pigs
Spay—To render a female incapable of reproduction
Suidae—A family of the order Artiodactyla
Sus—A genus of the family Suidae
Sus scrofa—A species of the genus *Sus*; a pig, hog, or boar
Ungulate—Any animal that has hooves
Weaner—A piglet only recently weaned from its mother's milk

Associations and Registries

INTERNATIONAL POTBELLY PIG REGISTRY (IPPR)
PO Box 277
Pescadero, CA 94060

NATIONAL COMMITTEES ON POTBELLIED PIGS (NCOPP)
10717 Citrus Drive
Moorpark, CA 93021

NORTH AMERICAN POTBELLIED PIG ASSOCIATION (NAPPA)
PO Box 90816
Austin, TX 78709-0816

POTBELLIED PIG REGISTRY SERVICE, INC. (PPRSI)
22819 Stanton Road
Lakeville, IN 46536
(Includes the former American Miniature Pig Registry, Georgia)

Suggested Reading

T.F.H. offers two additional books on the pot-bellied pig. *Pot-Bellied Pigs and other Miniature Pet Pigs,* by Lisa Hall Huckaby consists of 143 pages containing an overview of information from the origin of pot-bellies to the different breeds of miniature pigs, as well as information on general care. With over 80 beautiful full-color photographs, this book offers the future pig owner valuable information on what to expect from these endearing pets.

Pot-bellied Pigs As Your New Family Pet, by Michael Taylor contains 192 pages of information and over 80 full-color photographs on the increasingly popular pot-bellied pig. This book will provide you with information ranging from purchasing a pig, to breeding, to exhibition. This book is a must for any pot-belly owner.

T.F.H. offers books not only on pot-bellied pigs but also on almost all other pet animals, fish, reptiles, and amphibians as well. Many of these titles are available from the same place you purchased this publication. For information on the many other various titles available, write to us for a free catalogue at:

T.F.H. Publications
One T.F.H. Plaza
Third & Union Avenues
Neptune, N.J. 07753

Index